Do Better!
Be Better!

You Don't Have To.
YOU GET TO!

Do Better! Be Better!

You Don't Have To. YOU GET TO!

by

Mark D. Estes

Copyright © 2023, Mark D. Estes

All rights reserved. Printed in the U.S.A.

No part of this publication may be reproduced or transmitted in any form or by any means, electronic or mechanical, including photocopy, recording or any information storage and retrieval system now known or to be invented, without permission in writing from the publisher, except by a reviewer who wishes to quote brief passages in connection with a review written for inclusion
in a magazine, newspaper or broadcast.

Quantity Purchases:
Companies, professional groups, clubs, and other organizations may qualify for special terms when ordering quantities of this title.
For information, email info@ebooks2go.net,
or call (847) 598-1150 ext. 4141.
www.ebooks2go.net

Published in the United States by eBooks2go, Inc.
1827 Walden Office Square, Suite 260, Schaumburg, IL 60173

ISBN: 978-1-5457-5665-2

Library of Congress Cataloging in Publication

Do Better! Be Better!

Dedicated to my mom and dad who showed me many ways to do better and be better and to my wife, Evelyn, who inspires me to do so.

Contents

Introduction xi

Why Do or Be Better? 1

What Do You Want? 7

The Key to Your Success Is Your Attitude 15
    Attitude Is Everything 15
    Paradigm: Shift Your Paradigm to
    Change Your Attitude 17

Make It Real 22
    Setting Goals: Turning Your Dreams into Reality 22

Start Doing Better 28
    How Do You Go About Doing Better and Being Better? 28
    Inspiration and Wisdom from Successful People 30

Steps for Doing Better 33
    Stop Doing the Wrong Things 34
    Start Doing the Right Things 36
    What Will You Do and When? 38

Universal Truths 43
    Work over Time Is Power 43
    Why Do People Act? 45
    The Business of Business Is People 51

Do Better By Choice 55

Dealing Better with Crises 63
    Some Firsthand Experience with Crises 63
    Tools and Tactics for Dealing Better with Crises 66
    Crisis and Opportunity 71
    Why Do Bad Things Happen? 73

Doing More; Doing Better 77
    If You Could Do It Again, How Would
    You Do It Better? 80
    Do Better, but Don't Expect Perfection 86
    Take Responsibility and Authority 87

Do Better with Balance 91

Have a Better Quality of Life 96

Do Better by Being More Optimistic 103

Find More Inspiration and Motivation to Do Better 110

Boost Your Willpower 116

Stop Procrastinating 122

Using Your Gifts to Do Better in Your Roles 129
    Things to Do to Be a Better 131

Helping Others in Your Roles 136

Doing Something to Move Forward. 142
    Ideas for Doing Better 144
    Falling off the Wagon 147
    Some Grammar Tips 148

Additional Inspiration and Wisdom from Others 151

Conclusion 165

Appendices. 171
    Appendix 1—Talents People Have 171
    Appendix 2—Good Deed Ideas 181

Endnotes. 186

Introduction

- Why do you want to do better?
- What do you want?
- Don't be afraid to dream big!
- You can do better!
- Want it, work for it, get it!

Good for you for looking at this book and thinking about doing better and being better! You have made it this far in life and have a lot more you can achieve. You have tremendous abilities to make things happen, achieve greatness, benefit society, and to be happy! This book exists for your benefit. These pages contain knowledge, skills, tactics, insights from hundreds of people, lifetimes of learning, and wisdom gained from countless lessons learned from failures by others—all for you. You can build on the wisdom from others and be an enormous success! All it takes on your part is desire, defining what you want and when you want it, time, effort, and a willingness to make mistakes and learn from them. Success does not mean all hard work, then reward. It is a wonderful process and journey from where you are to where you want to be. Getting there includes a lot of hard work, but it is meaningful work with a purpose toward dreams and goals. Your dreams, goals, and desires are all within your control. I promise you that you will learn some new things, be reminded of some things you already know, and be able to do better and be better! How much better depends on how much you want.

This book contains information collected to help you be inspired to want to do better, help you to be motivated for you to take the steps to be better, and provide you some of the tools available to help you do better and be better. I am no more special or greater than you. I have spent a large part of my life trying to do better, learning from successful people, listening to audio programs on doing better, attending seminars, and reading books about doing better and learning from trial and error. I envision you finding some insights and inspiration from this book to make a positive change to your own life. As part of that positive change, I hope you share insights from the book, and the book itself, with others.

I apologize if some of my stories or examples might not all resonate with you, but I hope that some do. I have read books in which the authors spend a lot of time glorifying themselves and/or go on about a bunch of extraneous personal information. I, on the other hand, tend to be too blunt at times. Somewhere in between there is a reasonable balance that I hope I have portrayed in this book and that it works for you. My wife, Evelyn, has been my major inspiration for trying to do better and be better. She deserves the very best I can be, and I am proud to have made some progress doing better with her as my inspiration. She is my muse, my best friend, my soul mate, and a large part of my reason for wanting to do better and be better. Even though I am blessed with having my muse, it has taken me decades to getting around to writing this book and to making some significant progress on some of my other goals. Parts of this book will likely seem a little over the top with positive, hopeful, upbeat, and encouraging messages. While you have likely heard some of this before, I expect there is still more and better that you want to accomplish that you haven't for some reason been able to do. Maybe if I had read the right book decades ago I would have been inspired to get more of my goals accomplished earlier in life. I hope you will find some inspiration, motivation, and wisdom that helps you do better and be better, or at least do so faster!

What are your reasons to do better? Do you have children who deserve you at your best? A spouse, significant other, friend, or someone else who makes you want to do better and be better? With whom will you share your stellar success when you decide to achieve it? How about you? Don't you deserve the best from the world around you and from you yourself? You have a greatness in you and can accomplish wonderous things! You are so unique that you are the only one, for better or worse, who can really change you. While that can seem somewhat scary and a huge responsibility for you, it is awesome that you alone have control over you! You have the wonderful power to shape your future by creating ideas, making decisions, and doing things!

Whoever or whatever it takes, embrace the inspiration and motivation that fans the spark of greatness in you to the level of a smoldering ember, then a long-lasting flame of continued greatness. Warm those around you, and be a light for others. The good news is that you don't have to wait for someone else to try to change you, to give you desire and a will to succeed. You have all that within you. Find your inspirations to bring them to the surface and make them real. Continuously feed your inspiration, especially in times of difficulty, when it is needed most. Learn and use tools to continue making progress, even when your short-term motivation fades.

People have been doing great things for thousands of years and learning lessons sometimes at high personal cost. While there has never been and will never be another you, with your dreams, hopes, abilities, and challenges, people have been facing the same adversity for a long time. Today there is so much easy access to information and platforms to connect with others. You can learn about the lives, efforts, success, failures, and lessons learned from great people who have done similar things to what you want to do. You don't have to search through hundreds of books and thousands of pages at the library. You don't have to spend twenty years interviewing people. All you have to do is type, point, click, or just say what you want to learn from the internet. Ralph Waldo Emerson[1] wrote, back in the 1800s, about a "collective consciousness" that is a universal mind from which an individual can understand "all that is or can be done." In his book *Think and Grow Rich*, from the 1930s, Napoleon Hill[2] mentions an "infinite intelligence" that we can tap into by visualizing our goals and having strong desires to achieve them. I don't want to trivialize either man's great philosophical theories, but don't we have that now with the internet? Moreover, aren't we today pretty much all connected with cell phones, computers, email, social media, TV, and radio?

Isn't this a magical time in which we live! You have access to more ideas, support, knowledge, wisdom, opportunities, and tools to achieve them than in any time in our history. Many of these tools have come into being only in the last couple of decades. How will you take advantage of all this wonderous new technology and connectivity? What do you want? Based on all my research and experience, the most important factor for success is a strong desire. Without it, there is no inspiration, motivation, or driving force to make things happen. I don't know you. I don't know what you want or what sparks your soul. If you can find a dream, desire, or heart song and work hard for it, good for you. Let the world watch out, because nothing will keep you from your success!

Not only after your success will you be able to help others with their needs, wants, and dreams, if you so choose, but also during your process of becoming successful by meeting others' needs. The better you provide goods, services, and benefits for others, the better you are compensated. The better you are compensated, the more you can address your needs, wants, and dreams. A few times in this book, I make references to engineering, physics, or science, partly because of my engineering education and partly because there are certain laws or truths that apply both to scientific principles and general life principles. To start, the first law of thermodynamics regarding conservation of energy, loosely interpreted, states, "You can't get something for nothing." In terms of general life principles, "You have to give a little to get a little. If you give a lot, you get a lot." In other words, the more people you provide benefit to, the more benefit you get. While another interpretation of the first law is that because energy is finite you have to take from others in order to gain because resources and wealth are limited, both of which I believe do not apply to life, well-being, goodness, mental energy, or happiness. You definitely don't have to take anything from others in order to be happy! On the contrary, the happier you are, the happier you can help others be.

This book is laid out in order for you to do better and be better, starting with why, then what and when, then how, then doing even better. There is a section at the end with inspiration and wisdom quotes from notable people with a brief biography of each person. There is also an appendix of talents and gifts people have and a list of good deeds that might give you some ideas for how you can be better by doing good for the sake of good. You will see mentioned in this book that as you provide goods, services, and help to others, you succeed and are able to reach your goals and dreams. It is the way our world works. Taking from others in order to succeed lasts only so long, until the well runs dry, and there is nothing left to take. The real way to build yourself up is not to tear others down but with mutual benefit. The one you have the most control over is you. As you build your dreams, work toward your goals, and pursue your ambitions, you will undoubtedly be inspired and assisted by others. In kind, you can inspire and assist others.

As you make your way through this book, I suggest that you keep a notepad and pencil or pen nearby so you can take notes. You might want to remember or refer to some of the content, but more importantly you might want to write down your thoughts about why, what, or how you want to do things better and be better. There are also some lists and things suggested that you might want to write down. One way to make ideas, dreams, and goals more real is to write them down. I have included many references to songs in this book. Originally, I wanted to reprint the lyrics themselves but found that I cannot legally do so. We can find in songs inspiration and food for thought about life and wisdom to consider. They say that art imitates life, or is it the other way around?

I am excited for you, the opportunities that you have to do better and be better, and hope that this book will help you. I wish that in my youth I had the knowledge and wisdom I have learned from life and from others that I have now and shared with you in this book. Unfortunately, the only way we learn is from personal experience and from the experiences of others in person or from the books containing their knowledge and wisdom. If you decide to do better and be better, you are already on track to do so. I hope this book gives you some inspiration, motivation, tools, and tactics to help you in your efforts. You have awesome potential! You can do as much better as you want to. The knowledge and wisdom of the ages is at your fingertips! It is all up to you!

Why Do or Be Better?

- If you shoot for the stars and settle for the moon, you still made it pretty far!
- Ancient proverb: the best time to plant a tree was twenty years ago; the next best time is today.
- You are never too old to change, learn, or succeed!
- You are the master of your own destiny!
- It is with righteous indignation that I vow to make up for my lack of success to date by getting better and doubling my efforts to succeed.

The driving force behind you doing better is your desire to do so. If you don't already have a strong desire to do better, or want a potential reminder why you want to do and be better, you can review the items listed later in this chapter, which might trigger or reinforce some inspiration or motivation for you. Don't be shy about it. Don't judge whether you can accomplish it, it looks too hard, or you don't deserve it. Just pick a dream or two and let yourself imagine attaining what you want. Let yourself desire something better than you have now. Don't let fear of failure, feeling unworthy, or lack of faith in yourself keep you from wanting and desire to do better and have more.

I have been guilty of not pursuing my dreams because of fear and a lack of desire. I had let my desire remain stifled, at times feeling unworthy of success. I don't know. Maybe thousands of times I have gone to bed thinking: *I will get up early tomorrow and start working on goals*, then feel defeated for not doing so. Inspiration can be fleeting. Motivation can be fragile. In this book, you will find tools to keep you moving forward, including maintaining a positive attitude, defining what you want, writing things down, documenting steps to take, doing the right things, dealing better with crises, dealing better with people, and learning from others. Your foundation to learn, keep moving forward, and do better for yourself, especially in the face of hardships and setbacks, is your desire, your belief in yourself, and your hope for better outcomes. Even when you aren't thinking of your desire, your belief in yourself is low, and your hope seems to be fading, there are tools and tactics to keep you moving. To get started, why do you want to do better?

How many times have you thought about:

- Some celebrity or other apparently successful person and said to yourself, "Why does that person seem to have it all?"
- The next-door neighbors with kids, a dog, a pool, and a garage, always looking perfect and happy
- The kid you see driving the Porsche his parents gave him who speeds through a residential neighborhood
- The professional athlete with his bright future and arrogant attitude
- The coworker with half your skills doing better than you, who brags about how great he is
- The times when you think back about all your hopes and dreams when you were young that are unfulfilled
- The dreams that you still have but don't know how to make happen
- The end of the day, when you think, *Is this all there is for me?*
- *Someday I will ...* but never do
- The things you want to do to do better but have been afraid to try or start
- The things have you started in the past but never followed through

- The short-term sting of past failures that blinded you to the lessons you learned from trying
- The times when you feel you don't deserve better; maybe you have done harm to others emotionally or otherwise; you feel angry or frustrated with where you are at in life and don't know what to do but know that you want something
- How you are excited at times about all the opportunities out there, but do not know where to start
- That you are doing well, making lots of money, and have lots of things but feel hollow and without purpose sometimes
- What you want to do as a career
- Atoning for a lot of bad you have done
- *Why does life have to be so hard?*
- How you deserve better
- Being on the precipice of greatness
- It being time you started doing better

It is natural to at times to feel somewhat reluctant to have dreams and goals for fear of not reaching them, being disappointed, and/or otherwise failing. We can worry about what others might think of us if we fail. We can be worried that after putting in a lot of hard work we still don't achieve what we wanted. The reality is that all the doubt and fear you can think of are based on fictitious maybes—they're not real. Yes, you might have some setbacks from which you will learn. Yes, you might change course during pursuit of a dream, maybe even for a better dream. Yes, you will face some challenges for which you will become better in order to overcome. Most of all, yes, you will know that your efforts have meaning, and you should be proud of yourself for trying!

What would you do better if you could go back in time and do it again? Well, sorry that is not going to happen. The awesome thing is that all of the experiences good and bad that you have had so far because of your efforts has made you a better, stronger, wiser person for you today and you in the future. Think about how much better you will be in the future if you want to, decide to, and make the effort? Consider the potential snowball effect of you wanting something, working toward it—maybe having a few setbacks from which you learn—working smarter and getting what you want. Once you do that with one small thing, why not try something bigger? Why not try more things? Once you start getting some experience, knowledge, additional confidence, and momentum on a successful path, you will be even more effective and get more of what you want.

Life is a journey. Where you go, how far you go, and how much you enjoy it is up to you. You may feel that you are perfectly happy in your current situation with no desire to change even for the better. Is that really the case, or are you afraid that admitting otherwise would leave you exposed to trying for better and potential disappointment and feeling like a failure? Are you in a rut (comfortable or otherwise)? I have heard that a rut is just a grave with the ends knocked out. Throughout this book you will find ideas, statements, thoughts, and guidance I have found from learning from others in the past, current research online, and from my own experience. While your situation is as unique as you, almost everything you do, have faced, or want to do, someone else has likely experienced, faced, or done something similar. Because you are reading this book, you have come to the realization that you don't know everything. You can either be afraid of that fact or grow from understanding it. Just look at the wonderous things others have achieved from philosophy and art to technology and science. All of our achievements have come from someone's desire to do something better or something new.

Do you remember the dreams of your youth? What about the desire for more that you felt back when you were younger before the weight of responsibility, challenges, and setbacks piled up and weighed you down? Everyone, yes even you, are entitled to want more and better! Let yourself dream, want, hope, and expect great things. Your only real obstacle to achieving everything you want is you! No other person is going to change you. You can't change someone else. The great news is that you can change yourself, and others can change themselves! As in the song from Lee Ann Womack, "I Hope You Dance," which I often sing a portion of and dance to with my wife, I hope you get the most out of life. If you are not doing better, you are doing worse. If you don't improve, you are doing worse than you can be. There is always room for improvement. You can always do more, do better, and be better!

Let yourself want, desire, be optimistic, and hope. You can stay the same, stay still, be safe from disappointment, and not try, but where is the fun in that? No guts, no glory! It is the ups and downs that make life interesting and fun. Let that spark of desire light your hope! How many times does it take for you to be set back, have a failure, not meet your expectations, take a risk, and lose before you never want to hope or try again? That is one of those traps or trick questions that does not have to have any real meaning unless you give it one. That question is a good example of concentrating on or working on the wrong end of the problem. From a philosophical or logical view, the question is baseless because it is based on the premise that after some amount of failures, setbacks, or disappointments, you are supposed to give up or quit trying. Says who? If the Wright brothers had given up after the first few tries, they would have not invented the airplane! If Thomas Edison had given up after the first 4,500 tries, we wouldn't have the light bulb. If Babe Ruth, Michael Jordan, Tom Brady, or other star athletes had given up after a few setbacks, how far would they have made it? Don't let yourself get trapped into some BS preconception invented by you or anyone else to let you off the hook for having desires, dreams, goals, and aspirations and believing you can achieve them! I expect that some of what I have written in this book may sound like over-the-top attempts to tug at your heart strings or otherwise help you be inspired or motivated to do better and be better. Bear with me though because this is important. Your desires, dreams, goals, and aspirations will drive you forward toward doing better and being better.

If you let yourself desire something enough and are willing to put the work into achieving it, then look out world—nothing is going to stop you. It will be easier and faster if you avail yourself of some of the knowledge, tactics, and wisdom in this book and from other sources. If you learn from your setbacks, keep your heart focused, and believe, you can do almost anything. One task at a time. One day at a time. Each step brings you closer.

I have included throughout this book tools and tactics for you to do better and to help you feel more confident with your ability to succeed. From your attitude, to a better understanding of how things happen and why, to dealing better with crises, to maintaining optimism, inspiration and motivation, willpower, and wisdom from others, there is a tremendous amount of information and thoughts that can help you do better.

Chapter Summary

- Why do you want to do better?
- Let yourself have a strong desire.
- Desire will drive your success.
- You will learn from any setbacks and obstacles.
- There are tools to keep you going, even when motivation fades.

What Do You Want?

- You have enormous potential to succeed!
- You have the power to do better and be better!
- Pick your destination in order to know which direction to go!
- Make progress now by writing down what you want!
- Let your desire fuel your success!

What do you want? This is probably the most important question you can answer. Be specific. Maybe start with a list. What are your dreams? What big and small changes in your life do you want to see happen? This is it. This is your chance to choose. I implore you to look deep inside yourself if you have to. Try to remember dreams you had when you were young. Write them down! Understand it is normal if you are reluctant because it feels like a silly exercise. You don't have to show anyone. It takes courage to decide, to choose, to want, to risk disappointment, to try, and to risk failure. Without some failure, there is no appreciation of success. From all small failures come the lessons needed to succeed. You don't have to start from scratch. You have this book and the knowledge and wisdom acquired over years of learning from other books and personal experience, including the awesome access to information on the internet.

This is the good stuff about life! It is not that you have to do any of this. It is that you get to! Don't miss out! As the Nike slogan says: "Just Do It!" Do it now! What is *doing* better to you? What is *being* better to you?

You can start by brainstorming and writing down things that you want. By writing them down, they become more real, and you can build on them.

What I want most is:

_____

_____

_____

_____

Other things I want include:

_____

_____

_____

_____

The time frames I want things to happen include:

_____

_____

_____

_____

The reasons I want these things are:

_____

_____

_____

_____

Did you write a real big would-be-awesome-when-you-make-it-happen goal? If you had one that would be the best, above all others, what would it be? Is it big? Is it big enough to scare you? I hope for you that it is big enough to scare you. In that case, it must really be worthy of you.

Assuming you wrote something, good job! If you did not, maybe you will at some point. If nothing comes to mind, or even if you just want some other ideas to think about, take a look at the list of sample goals and sample big or scary dreams and goals of the type that I am referring to that you can achieve:

Sample goals include:

- learn a new language;
- lose thirty pounds of unneeded weight;
- get a certain, better, or any job;
- change careers;
- buy a house (or buy a bigger house);
- be a better parent;
- be more positive; or
- relocate.

Sample big, scary, and noble goals include:

- mentor someone to greatness;
- create a hugely successful business;
- write the next great American novel;
- direct and/or produce a movie;
- have or adopt a child and be a good parent;
- teach and inspire others for greatness;
- cure a disease; or
- become a billionaire.

During a recent internet search, I found the following list of the top-twenty goals of Americans for the year:

1. get finances in order
2. get out of debt
3. learn something new
4. get more organized
5. buy a new home
6. exercise more
7. spend more time with family and friends
8. travel more
9. do something nice for myself
10. learn a new skill
11. buy a new car
12. lose weight
13. volunteer more often
14. disconnect from technology
15. remodel my home
16. quit my vices
17. redecorate my home
18. cook more frequently
19. organize closet
20. bring a pet into the family

Not everyone's top goals rise to the level of big, scary, or noble goals, but to each their own. I wanted to show this list to help spur your imagination and for you to possibly feel better about your goal(s).

The other list I found online recently is the top-ten things people around the world wish for:

1. happiness
2. freedom
3. peace

4. sex
5. fame
6. to change ourselves
7. love
8. the fundamentals (food, shelter, medical treatment)
9. money
10. good health

I find in this list some larger, arguably more meaningful items, but they are shown as wishes, not goals. The distinction being that wishes imply things just happening, while goals imply taking responsibility and authority to make them happen yourself. I find it very encouraging that the top dream listed is happiness! Of all the dreams and goals listed above, happiness is the one most within our immediate control. Happiness is a state of mind and attitude. We own and have immediate control over our own attitudes; therefore, we have immediate control over our happiness. Yes, it is that simple! I said simple, not necessarily easy. The following chapters offer some insights, tools, and tactics to have better control over our attitudes and being happy.

Your dreams and goals are the reason for this book. What you want is your definition of what is better. I hope you can learn some insights from this book on how you can do better and be better to realize your dreams.

Write down a list of your dreams. Give yourself a time frame or deadline for each dream. This will help turn them into goals and let you know when you need to get certain steps done in order to achieve the end results. Target dates are a great way to keep you from procrastinating and staying on Someday Isle. If you miss a target date, try not to beat yourself up. You are still likely a lot closer than you were.

Some sample target for goals might be:

- Learn a new language within twelve months.
- Lose thirty pounds of unneeded weight within six months.
- Get a certain, better, or any job within three months.

Larger goals might include longer time frames, such as:

- Have or adopt a child within five years.
- Cure a disease within ten years.
- Become a billionaire by the age of forty.

Again, for each of your goals or dreams, it is your desire or why you want these things to happen that will be your driving force behind your success. As you go through the hard work of laying out plans, getting things done, learning from failed attempts, and overcoming hardship, it is your why, your desire, and the fire in your heart that will keep you going. The following show some desires, or whys, for goals:

- Learn a new language within twelve months so you can have a better time when you go to France next year for two months as planned.
- Lose thirty pounds of unneeded weight within six months because your doctor told you that you are at high risk for heart disease because of being overweight, and you are sick of being out of breath when hiking or playing sports.
- Get a certain, better, or any job within three months because you need more, or any, income to keep your house or get a better one.
- Have or adopt a child within five years because you value family so highly and know you would be a great parent.
- Cure a disease within ten years so that no one has to suffer with the same disease that killed your sibling at a young age.
- Become a billionaire by the age of forty years old so that you can devote your wealth to making the world a better place and to end child hunger.

You have already done better by starting to read this book and writing down your dreams. In the next chapters, I will share insights and tools to help you realize your dreams by turning them into achievable goals. There will be some exercises and tasks that I recommend to help you. If it looks like what I suggest might work for you, great. If you have other ideas that will work better, use those. If you can find something else on the internet that you think is better, use that. The important things are to define what you want to do, figure out what you need to get what you want done, track your progress, and keep yourself on track with getting things done, even if your motivation wavers at times. No more waiting, no more "someday I will." The only one you need to really answer to is you.

The good news is, you have control over how you are doing, what you achieve, and how happy you are. While how you are doing and what you achieve may take some significant effort and time, the great news is happiness is within your immediate control, as you will see in the next section. Why is that important? Think about it. Are we happy because we achieve success, or do we succeed because we are happy? I am not sure if the answer is that simple. In any event, if we spend most of our time working on the journeys to success, it stands to reason that we want to be happy during the process, not just at the end. Also, with success, is that really the end? Will you really just stop, or will you continue moving forward, doing better, and reaching new goals?

Identifying and choosing what you want and how you want to do better is the first step in any journey to success. If you don't have a purpose for what you do, does it matter what you are doing? If you have specific dreams and goals, you are much more likely to achieve them than if they are not specific and definitely not likely if you don't have them in the first place. It might seem comfortable having no real desires or goals, but do you ever feel that you might me missing out? Isn't real living wanting things, taking chances, working toward things and achieving success? It can be scary to hope for something, dream, and consider moving from your low-risk comfort zone. Keep in mind that the risk you have with not wanting and trying for more creates the risk of losing out on life and lost opportunity. Most people look back and wish they had tried to do more. It is rare that we look back and think: *I wish I had never tried that new adventure or opportunity*!

Let yourself dream, hope, and want. Balance the risk of never fulfilling your potential against the risk of short-term failure. After all, this is your life, make what you want of it. You pick and own your desires, what you want, and when you want them. Revel in the power of your choices and your ability to make things happen. Do better working toward them and be better in the process!

Chapter Summary

- Pick your goals, your dreams, your destination.
- Feel free to dream big!
- Set time frames for when you want to have things happen.
- Track your progress and let it motivate you.
- Choose your dreams, let your heart want, and enjoy your progress and successes!

The Key to Your Success Is Your Attitude

- If you want to be happy, it is all up to you!
- Happiness is an attitude and within your control!
- Count your blessings!
- Look at all the opportunities in front of you!
- Life is too short to not be happy now!

Attitude Is Everything

When I just looked up the definition of *happiness* online, I found "the state of being happy." For example: "She struggled to find happiness in her life." Are you someone who is as happy as you could possibly be? Are you someone who feels that you struggle to find happiness in your life? I have great news for you! Happiness is a state of mind. We have immediate control over our state of mind. We, therefore, have immediate control over our happiness! Our control lies in our attitude and our ability to control our attitude.

Our attitude not only sets our state of mind and happiness but also affects our desires and abilities to function and succeed. Hope is a product of our attitude. If we have an attitude of potential positive outcomes, we have hope. If we don't have hope, how do we go forward doing anything? The good news is, you own your attitude. Other peoples' actions, occurrences in the world, your own decisions, and their effects all can influence your attitude only to the extent that you let them. If you are like many of us, controlling our attitude can be a struggle at times. There are tips, tactics, and things that you can do to aid you. A great tool in doing this is to frame how you see things, or your paradigm from which you see things. This next section includes some stories, examples, and tools I hope you find helpful in the all-important area of gaining control over your attitude.

Einstein had his theories of relativity. I have my own, which I call Estes's theory of relativity: no matter how bad things are for you, there is someone who has it worse. When I was twenty-five years old and going daily for radiation treatments for my brain tumor, there was a young boy, two to three years old, before me to whom they gave anesthesia so that he could stay still and tolerate his radiation treatments for a brain tumor. I had an already twenty-two-year head start on him and didn't feel much like I had a good reason to complain after seeing his situation.

There are many other examples much more inspiring than anything I have seen or done, including stories about Helen Keller, other challenged people, and their triumphs over adversity. The point is, we each have our own events and people in our lives who impact us, make us think, and help shape our attitudes.

There is a scene in a movie that I remember, which I think is from the movie *Batman v Superman: Dawn of Justice*. The setting is after Superman is dead from the previous movie, crime is rampant, and it apparently seems the director wanted to show there is little or no hope for society. A homeless-looking young to middle-aged man, as I remember, is sitting on the ground among debris with a cardboard sign marked: "I TRIED." I remember when I first saw this I thought, *Okay, I guess I feel sorry for him and people like him in similar situations who tried, failed, and gave up*. Wouldn't that be a great solution to my own troubles and hardships? Give up and say, "I tried."

Since then, however, the more I think about that scene, the more I am resolved not to be one who gives up, blaming difficult situations or other people. I have my negative thoughts, feelings of despair, and discouragement, but I have resolved to continue and wrestle my attitude back to positive, productive thoughts with the tools I have built for myself and learned from others. If I can do this as a relatively nonsocial middle-aged married man with limited contacts, think of how much better you can do with a better attitude and some goals!

I am still working on doing better and being better with a better attitude myself. I know that I have come a long way but can still do better. Our attitude can be a fickle, sensitive thing if we let it, but you can turn your attitude around completely and develop a positive attitude as a habit.

One of the great ways to improve your attitude is do positive things. Take action. Do something that moves you closer to your goals—actually do some of the things that you said you will do. Later in this book, you will see some suggestions on how to list and track your progress as you get things done. Consider that accomplishing a large goal consists of accomplishing a lot of smaller goals within your immediate control. As you make progress and get things done, you are having successes. Even if you have some setbacks or encounter some obstacles, you are learning and getting prepared to do better.

Paradigm: Shift Your Paradigm to Change Your Attitude

One of the books I read recently talked about the importance of paradigm.

In his book *The Seven Habits of Highly Effective People*, author Stephen R. Covey discusses the term *paradigm shift* and its potential impact on our attitude. I had read the book years ago and do not remember if I picked up the concept from this book or elsewhere, but I know I use the concept often. As I understand it, *paradigm* means how you see something based on the surrounding circumstances or framing, and *paradigm shift* means a change in how you see something based on your changed understanding of the surrounding circumstances.

A few examples of paradigm shift include:

You see someone on the highway driving fast and recklessly in an out of traffic and think, *What a self-centered jerk.* How would your attitude change if you learned that the driver had his three-year-old daughter in the car who was having an allergic reaction to a beesting, could barely breathe, and needed to get to the hospital right away for a chance to live?

It's like yelling at your dog for barking at the outside window and the realizing there was someone in your yard. Stephen Covey's example is of a man with rambunctious, out-of-control kids at a train station, which is very annoying to you, until you find out his wife, their mom, just died, and they are on their way back from the hospital.

Why is the paradigm so important? In essence, it is the framing around which you view the world or specific item at hand and sets your perspective or how you see things. If you start out thinking you will have a lousy day, chances are no matter what happens you will have a lousy day. On the other hand, if you start out thinking you will have an awesome day, you likely will see and appreciate the positives.

We all know people who are often negative and see things as bad or worse. My wife has, on occasion, asked if her imperfections or struggles at times are too much for me to want to handle. My usual response is that sometimes she is like a suitcase full of money—difficult to carry at times but definitely worth the effort.

I recently read a new perspective on the glass-half-full versus glass-half-empty example of paradigm. The current accepted understanding of this analogy is that optimistic people see the glass as half full, while pessimistic people see the glass as half empty. I suppose we cannot ignore the disturbed individual who might also see a container of fluid that you can splash into someone's eyes to temporarily blind them while you break the glass on the table to use as a weapon to hurt the person you blinded. The new spin I found refreshing is that it is just a glass you can refill!

If you think about it, people react to paradigm framing, or perspective, in different ways. Let's say you wake up in the morning, and the first thing you do is stub your toe. Next, you go to brush your teeth and drop the toothpaste, which hits your toe. You go to the kitchen, and the dog has left you a big, nasty present in the middle of the floor. You get into a car accident on the way to work. You get to work, and a coworker says, "Good morning. How's the world treating you?"

You have a choice of how you respond. The glass-half-empty paradigm person might say, "Awful!" followed by the list of things that have gone wrong.

The glass-half-full person might say, "Any day above ground is a good day."

The darker sense of humor person might say, "The world is treating me like a baby's diaper," which I think is a line from the TV show *Cheers*.

Yet another response could be, "Better than I deserve." The great thing about it is, you get to choose how you respond and what you say. Keep in mind that your answer in some small way will frame your coworker's attitude and impression of you.

What we say and how we say it to other people not only affects their perception of us but also our own self-perception and attitude. What we say to or about ourselves also has great impact on our attitude and ensuing level of success. If you do not believe in yourself, who will?

While I listen to a lot of different music, including some alternative and heavy metal—that includes questionably appropriate lyrics and themes—I do draw the line sometimes. For example, I do turn down or off the still popular song from the 1990s by the artist Beck titled "Loser." While I like the song, multiple times he sings about being not so great. Again, I am no purist when it comes to what I listen to or watch, but this is too much. I simply choose not to listen to this song. I suggest that you draw your own lines and stick to them based on your own assessments. Keep in mind also that your children likely won't have the same judgment to filter what they listen to and its impact.

I remember reading about and/or hearing an audio program about an entire study and practice of neurolinguistic programming. From what I recall, it covers communications content, such as songs and their ensuing impact on behavior. Feeding your mind with different thoughts impacts how you think and feel. One of the reasons to control your attitude is to make sure that you believe in yourself and in what you are doing. While it is no guarantee that you can accomplish everything you believe you can, you probably won't even try if you believe you can't. Sometimes we all need a little help with our attitudes or our paradigms. Other than sheer force of will, how do we change our paradigms, perspectives, and/or attitudes? Sometimes it helps to read inspirational quotes from others.

Along with the ancient proverb shown as a chapter starter, "The best time to plant a tree is twenty years ago. The next best time is today!" I have collected and continue to read quotes to help me with my attitude and motivation. I have included for you a list of fifty quotes, authors, and some background on the authors toward the end of the book.

See the following top five that jump out for me from a recent list of three hundred I found on the internet:

- "It's hard to beat the person that never gives up!"—Babe Ruth (former baseball great)
- "Great things are done by a series of small things brought together."—Vincent van Gogh (famous painter from the 1800s)
- "A formula for success: double your rate of failure …."—Thomas J. Watson (former IBM CEO)
- "Today is your opportunity to build the tomorrow you want!" —Ken Poirot (author and PhD cancer researcher)
- "If your dreams don't scare you, they are too small!"—Richard Branson (billionaire)

A recurring theme throughout inspirational quotes and success stories is desire plus hard work equals success. In order to keep working hard, you need the right attitude and specific things on which you can focus your efforts. Companies and other teams use things such as mission statements, vision statements, and slogans as reminders of their goals and often detailed, long thought-out business plans to define where they want to be in the future and how they plan to get there.

While you don't need elaborate formal plans to define your goals and how to achieve them, you do need to decide what you want and should write them down. When you write them down, you are making them real. The next chapter has some strategies to help you make your dreams and goals real and strategies for you to accomplish them.

Chapter Summary

- Happiness is an attitude.
- Attitude keeps you moving forward.
- You have control over your attitude.
- You can help control your attitude by understanding the paradigm and paradigm shift.
- You can also control your attitude with inspiration and wisdom from others.

Make It Real

Setting Goals: Turning Your Dreams into Reality

- If it is to be, it is up to me!
- There but for my choices go I.
- Will adversity grind you down or polish you?
- Old proverb: The man who says it cannot be done should not interrupt the one doing it!

In my early twenties, the company I was working for sent me to a seminar that was supposed to be about time management. To this day, I still use a daily planner and many of the skills I learned there. I may not be great at planning and prioritizing my day, but I do try to draft a to-do list daily, document future appointments, jot down important events for future reference, and have it all in one place so I don't have to remember. While it was quite some time ago, I still remember the tag line of the seminar: "Any Dream Will Do!"

While you can choose anything for a dream, keep in mind the way the world works is we benefit when we help and/or please others. From the celebrity movie star or professional athlete who entertains and pleases millions (a small amount each) to the brain surgeon who helps one person at a time with life-and-death issues, we are all compensated for the benefit we bring to others.

If you concentrate on the goods or services that help people, do better, do more, and you will succeed and the money will follow. I think that often people confuse large sums of money with success, while in fact the real success was all the benefit or help that was provided.

Look at your dreams. What is it that you want to do that would benefit or please people? What does success with that look like for you? What will tremendous success look like, and how will it help you? Again, is your dream big enough to scare you?

Can you turn your dream into a goal? Goals are dreams with a target date. A goal is like a targeted destination for a trip. There may be many ways to get there with detours and bumps in the road, and it may take a long time. If you truly want to get there, you will find a way.

How can you go about making your goal(s) happen when you haven't been able to do so yet?

- Learn to become better at the process.
- Keep motivated to do the hard work.
- Figure out what needs to be done.
- Accept failures along the way as learning experiences.
- Ask for help along the way.
- Continue to get better as you go.
- Help as many others as you can along the way.
- Strive for excellence in all that you do.
- Be your own worst critic while being your own biggest supporter!

What if your goal seems too big? Break it into smaller pieces that you can manage. There is an old saying: "How do you eat an elephant? One bite at a time!" Other old sayings include: "The journey of a thousand miles begins with a single step" and "Rome wasn't built in a day."

Not all of us, myself included, have a natural drive to succeed with innate motivation. Sometimes we may feel like life has beaten us into submission and accept mediocrity with getting by as our primary goal in life. At times, we may need to find ways to keep ourselves motivated and stay on track doing what we should to achieve our goals.

Whether your goal is to lose a certain amount of weight or to become the largest and best provider of (pick your goods or services) in the world, break you goal into manageable pieces that you can convert into daily goals. I have wanted to write a book for over twenty years. I have bought and read books about how to write a nonfiction book, drafted outlines, and written some portions of chapter samples. I am going to share with you the steps and tools that helped me through this process in the hope that parts or something similar might help you. Keep in mind that as I am writing this, I am in the midst of grinding out the words, which for me is a big daily accomplishment in and of itself.

You see, I have always been a huge procrastinator, putting off today what I can do tomorrow, which never got done. Back on the first day of seventh grade, I remember the school principal talking at an assembly about how bad procrastination is and how he was going to make sure we all learn how not to succumb to it. I guess they never got around to it, at least not for me. I even bought a book about dealing with procrastination years ago but never got around to reading it!

The things that I have done that have helped me include:

- learned about the process
- bought and read a book about how to write a nonfiction book
- researched online different sites and suggestions as to what steps to take
- found conflicting advice about either writing a book proposal with sample chapters only or writing the entire book first, the latter of which I followed
- researched again and read some inspirational quotes and sayings
- drafted a list of benefits of getting this book written and other goals I have
- decided to, based on research, have the book be about two hundred pages
- once I get going, maybe I can write one page per hour or about two hundred hours to draft the book
- realized if I can spend ten hours a week on drafting the book, it will take me about twenty weeks

- by the end of August, another fifteen weeks gets me close to the end of the year, so my target goal is to have a book draft by December 31
- ten hours a week for the book plus ten hours per week on other goals is twenty hours per week
- I work a full-time forty-hour-a-week job, so if I do two hours per weekday before work, that leaves me ten hours on the weekend or five hours each Saturday and Sunday
- originally my goal was thirty thousand words for the book, which I revised up to do forty thousand, which added a month; then after seeing how many book pages that came out to be I revised my word count goal to sixty thousand, which added another three months

During a week, if I want to free up some of the weekend, I can do two hours before work, one hour when I get home after work, get fifteen hours done during the week, and leave only five hours for the weekend, which I can split up or get done all in one day and have the other off. It is Friday morning 6:51 a.m. as I write this, and I am in my third week, for which I am on track for three hours per weekday.

You see, I cannot control how long it takes me to draft the book or even draft a page. I can have an overall target goal based on a reasonable estimate and the real achievable weekly goal of twenty hours per week and daily goals to make that happen.

This is real for me now and within my control. While my attitude and motivation may increase or decrease daily or hourly, if I keep my commitment—or close to it—each week, I can hopefully achieve my goal close to the deadline I set, or earlier.

This isn't the first time I have had some success with progress goals. Over the year and a half prior to this round of target setting, I had some success with waking up at least an hour early almost every day. This worked for a year or so. I got a lot done but eventually I would miss a day or two and fall back into procrastinating and self-criticizing, disappointed at my lack of motivation. At that time, I did not have a weekly target goal to help me.

Early in my career, I also had some great success for a few years with setting and achieving yearly, monthly, weekly, and daily goals in sales as the director of business development for a small-to-midsized commercial building construction company. While the sales profession has its own challenges, large expense long-term process sales, such as building construction project sales, has lead time, profitability, and competition aspects that present extra challenges.

While it was a team effort, I engineered the sales plan, target goals, process improvements, and weekly sales behavior goals to get us over a two-and-a-half-year period to 450 percent volume growth, average project size increase of 75 percent, and the president of the company achieved a $1 million in profit the last year I was there. While I made some extra money from performance bonuses, I decided to leave the company because of the stress on me and the impact on my marriage. Unfortunately, as the company grew, our resources were strained, and I was being told to make promises for project completion that we could not meet. Many of our clients were small-to-midsize companies with five to twenty employees, and their projects were huge investments for them with serious consequences if schedules and other expectations were not met.

As you can probably guess, I heard that after I left the company that all the commitments I was told to make and weren't met were considered my fault. Whatever.

In any event, my own personal, inconsequential drama aside, if even I can have success with the tactic of breaking larger goals into manageable weekly and daily behavior goals, imagine what you can do! For me, at this point, the fact that I wrote this book has me feeling positive about what I am doing and optimistic that I will be successful with helping others. I hope that as you make progress with daily and weekly goals it helps motivate you to continue. Keep in mind that you will undoubtedly encounter many failures and setbacks, which will be valuable learning experiences. They may sting, but it will help you to look back at all your successes to improve your attitude and keep moving forward. Even a setback can be progress. Think of it as a chance to refocus and learn a better way to go. Take some steps. Learn as you go. Let your progress snowball and increase with every positive step you make!

Chapter Summary

- Make your dream real.
- Set daily and weekly goals.
- Do the work.
- Give yourself credit for getting things done.
- Be inspired by your progress.

Start Doing Better

How Do You Go About Doing Better and Being Better?

- Better is in the eye of the beholder!
- Commit to doing better every day because you deserve it!
- It is your day, your hour, your minute, but you only have them once!
- Do better for a week, a month, a year, and see how far you go!
- Your future self deserves your best today!

Something about this process worked for me, and since you are reading this, hopefully something similar might work for you. Writing this book has been a dream of mine for over twenty years. Your dreams do not need to be large, complex, or recognized by others to be important.

You can want to be a better parent, better spouse, better student, better person, more successful, happier, or healthier, all of which are great dreams and goals. But in order to know if you are achieving what you want, you need to somehow quantify what it is you want. Otherwise, how do you know if you are making progress, reached your goal, or surpassed it? You can't really identify what you should do to be successful until you decide on or define what success is. How can you celebrate when you get there or when you are halfway there or twice as far as you originally hoped if you have not defined what *there* is?

Let's say you want to be a better parent. First, define what that means. What does be a better parent mean to you? Do you want to spend more time with your kids? If so, how much time? How much time specifically each week? When during the day—hopefully the same time of day—can you spend the time? In reality, keep in mind you are not really "spending time"; you are sharing it. Do you want to share time at night reading to a small child, helping an older child with homework, talking about their day, or maybe even playing a video game or two with them? How about, at any age, asking what their dreams and goals are? You may have heard it in the past but could probably use a refresher. If you haven't heard it yet, I recommend you listen to Harry Chapin's song "Cat's in the Cradle" from 1974. In it, a man neglects to share time with his son when he is growing up, and when the man gets older, his son does not have time for him. My summary does not do it justice. Again, listen and relisten to it if you have or plan to have kids, and think again about sharing time with them.

Put some metrics or measure into your goals. What does being a better parent, being rich, or being a great doctor mean? What steps do you need to do to accomplish them, and when do they need to be done? How are you going to stay motivated in the short term to do the things you need to? Define what you need to do, hold yourself accountable in the short term, and let that build your success in the long term.

What starts you through all your efforts and the setting of your goals in the first place? This is your inspiration. It's your reason for doing this. It's what Logan Stout calls in his *Grit Factor* book, "your why." Knowing and defining your "why" or reason for your goal is how you better determine whether you are succeeding and firing your passion to set the goal and behavior goals in the first place. Your "why" will also drive your "what" for your goals and your "how much" for your scale, metrics, or measures.

Your dream may be to be enormously wealthy or at least financially independent. Your goal may be to have a billion dollars by the time you are thirty years old. What is your why? When you were growing up did your family struggle financially for basic needs like food, clothes, and somewhere to live? Did you hate the way that made you feel and you never wanted to feel that way again? Do you want to leave a legacy for your children? Do you simply feel that you deserve it? Do you want the freedom to buy and do things that a billion dollars can provide?

Do you want to have the resources to make the world a better place? How many resources to do how much good?

Inspiration and Wisdom from Successful People

Sometimes it can inspire us to do better when we learn about the success of others. Last time I checked, there are about 550 billionaires in the United States. While there some who have made their money with hedge funds, of which I don't understand the benefit to society, many have provided a great amount of benefit, including Bill Gates (Microsoft), Elon Musk (Tesla), Jeff Bezos (Amazon), Oprah Winfrey (entertainment—Harpo Productions), and Michael Jordan (sports), to name a few. Another billionaire of note includes Austin Russell, the youngest billionaire as listed by Entrepreneur online at twenty-five years old (autonomous vehicles). Other business fields that have produced billionaires include car dealerships, real estate development, energy, agriculture, and beauty supplies.

I don't know the full extent of how each of them accomplished all their success, but I expect if you ask them, they would say it takes a dream, a lot of hard work, dealing with hardship and failure, and learning from their mistakes. I wish I knew more about what drove them internally to reach such high levels of success, but I will settle for what I can learn in general about inspiration, self-motivation, goals, tools, and tactics to succeed.

I dug in this a little bit and researched the six billionaires listed above. I found the following quotes and brief insights into their successes:

(1) Bill Gates, cofounder of Microsoft according to Inc. online[3]:

"Gates was obsessed with programming but knew his company could not grow to the scale he wanted so he had to learn to delegate and trust other people's ability to write software. The article I saw also mentioned that in order to grow, Gates had to learn to surrender responsibilities to others."

(2) Elon Musk, CEO of Tesla, SpaceX[4]

The richest man in the world at $222 billion at the time this book was written, from an article published and seen online from Entrepreneurs, said that his motivation to succeed is driven by: "There need to be things that inspire you."

About his goal to travel to Mars: "It's about believing in the future and thinking that the future will be better than the past. And I can't think of anything more exciting than going out there and being among the stars."

(3)   Jeff Bezos, CEO of Amazon[5]

Jeff Bezos said: "If you are good at course correcting, being wrong may be less costly than you think."

Also, in reference to growing to many products instead of the initial book business he said: "I decided I had to give it a shot. I didn't think I'd regret trying and failing. And I would always be haunted by a decision not to try. After much consideration, I took the less safe path to follow my passion, and I'm proud of that choice."

(4)   Oprah Winfrey, Harpo Productions from "The key to realizing a dream is to focus not on success but on significance—and then the small steps and little victories along your path will take greater meaning." a blog online and entrepreneur.com:[6]

From a very early age Oprah had the irrepressible will to become rich and famous and was convinced that she would succeed.

She regularly devoted her talk shows to topics that had her guests portrayed as "victims" but empowered them by giving them a strong sense of hope and had the audience support them.

(5)   Michael Jordan, sports[7]

Along with his desire to win he has stated: "I can accept failure; everyone fails at something. But I can't accept not trying."

Another of his quotes is: "I've missed more than nine hundred shots in my career. I've lost over three hundred games. Twenty-six times I've been trusted to take the game-winning shot and missed. I've failed over and over again in my life. And that is why I succeed."

(6) Austin Russell, the world's youngest new billionaire, 2020, age twenty-five, autonomous vehicles[8]

He is "just clear about life goals in general" and has said "a lot of it is timing." Reportedly from a video interview with *Forbes* "there has been a lot of blood, sweat and tears in this."

Do you see a pattern?

Have and obsess over goals, get better at the process, and above all else, try, work hard, learn from mistakes and failure, provide benefit to society, and succeed! From what I have found so far in researching successful people for this book, I found a lot of *what* they accomplished, *how* they accomplished it, but not so much *why*. I am talking about the real why. What gave them the inspiration, the motivation, and the perseverance? Someday I hope to do the research and hopefully interview as many very successful people as possible and find out the real *why* of what drove them. If you decide you want to be extremely successful, when you do, will you let me interview you?

For a larger list of inspirational and wisdom quotes from notable people, see the list of forty-eight people I have provided in the section titled Additional Inspiration and Wisdom from Others. Along with the quote and the author, you will also find a brief background on each person so you can have at least some sense of who they were or are. You will also see the source from which the information was taken and can research each person more if you want to.

Chapter Summary

- What is *doing better* to you?
- To do better, revisit your reasons for wanting to do better —your "why."
- Study and learn from others and how they succeeded.
- Find and emulate patterns of successful people to better succeed.
- See more inspirational and wisdom quotes at the end of the book.

Steps for Doing Better

- "We are what we repeatedly do. Excellence is then not an act but a habit."—Aristotle[9]
- To ruin someone, remove their obstacles.
- "Concentrate on how far you can go versus how fast you can get there."—author unknown
- Maintain unwavering faith in your ability to achieve.
- "Whatever the mind can conceive, it can achieve." —Napoleon Hill[10]

You don't need to draft a business plan in order to succeed. It does help though to think through the steps and actions you need to do to accomplish your goals. When you plan a car trip to a destination a thousand miles away, you might want to have an idea of how to get there. Of course, you can just set a destination with Google Maps or Waze and start driving and expect to get there when suggested by the navigation app, but that probably isn't all the information you might want. What will be some of your stops, your milestones? What are some of the things you will want to see along the way? Where will you find the services you need along the way?

Write down your dream, be specific, and give a target for when you would like to get there. You now have a goal. What are some of the things that need to happen or steps that you have to take in order for you to move closer to your goal? What are the specific activities that you can do in order to make progress? How are you going to go about doing those activities? What types of regular activities and habits are you going to implement to make this happen? How will you measure progress? What will be considered success with your steps? How do you go about doing better? Some of the "low-hanging fruit" or easy picked things include, first, stop doing the wrong things.

Stop Doing the Wrong Things

I understand it may seem like a lot of work in front of you after you start really thinking about making it happen, but isn't it awesome you are making progress on how you can do better and better, realizing you *can* do better?

What are the things you can start doing to move your goals forward? One of the books I read over the last few months as research for this book highlighted one of the best ways you can help move yourself forward is to stop doing the negative behaviors that are counterproductive to your success. Makes sense; it is a lot tougher to go forward when you have negatives dragging you back. If you think about it, a quick way to do more net positive things, and better, is to minimize or eliminate the negatives.

Some of the negative things that we do that impede our success are:

- putting things off or procrastinating (see the chapter Stop Procrastinating);
- finding things to do that are of much less importance to put off working on what you really should;
- bad habits, like sleeping later than need be (or not enough);
- doing things that you know you shouldn't do;
- starting a project and not following through;
- letting your attitude be affected too much by others or small things;
- remembering your failures often but your successes rarely;
- being reluctant to try again after a failure or series of failures;
- unhealthy or health-risking behaviors;
- associating with a crowd of people whose traits you don't admire or aspire to have;

- criticizing others or otherwise tearing them down;
- complaining about things not in your control;
- blaming others for your difficulties; and
- getting angry and raising your voice in anger.

If you want to look smart, stand around stupid people. If you want to become stupid, stay with them for some time. If you want to become smart, hang around with smart people for some time. You may have to suffer some short-term feelings of not feeling too smart at first, but in the long run, you will be smarter for it. The same goes with you and successful people. You know when staying around certain people drags you down and when others elevate you. It is your choice; do what you think is best.

Another bad habit to consider is stop blaming others for things that are within your control. It may be true that others have wronged you or put obstacles in your way. Ultimately, we are responsible for our own success. Isn't it strange how you hear about so many self-made successful people but never hear about the self-made failures.

Your job is to get over being wronged and find ways around those obstacles. Feel free to remind yourself: "If it is to be, it is up to me." We are the product of our choices and our efforts. Others can help or hurt us along the way, but when it comes down to it, we own our situations. That is not to say that random difficulties or tragedies are our fault. How we deal with them is up to us. I still remember attending a support group for medical patients with various different problems. The facilitator of the group was a medical doctor. He talked in terms of attitude affecting our situations and alluded to the notion that if someone has cancer, it is their fault because of their poor attitude. I didn't say anything at the time, as I was much younger than he was, but I wish I did. How dare he tell someone they brought their own cancer or other sickness upon themselves! I wonder what his answer would have been if I asked him why an infant developed a deadly cancer.

From a book my wife bought me for my research, *Change Your Brain Change Your Life* by psychiatrist Daniel G. Amen, MD, I read that he labels automatic negative thoughts as ANTs that you can stomp out.

ANTs include thoughts such as "I can't do that," "I'm stupid," "It's too hard," or "No one ever gives me a chance." This type of statement when thought or spoken can feel crippling and comes from the one with the most control over your attitude, motivation, and success—you! How do you stomp the ANTs? Concentrate on the positive things you have done. Keep a list nearby of things you have accomplished that make you feel successful. In case you find yourself thinking or saying something negative automatically, you can do what I do, which is think or say "sometimes" afterward, softening the impact.

Stop letting others bring you down with their judgment, criticism, pessimism, and nasty thoughts. If someone tried to pour poison down your throat, would you let them? What about when they poison your mind with negative, such as you can't do it, you are unworthy, you have good excuses for not trying, your idea is stupid, and similar comments? Will you just let them keep working toward killing your dreams, goals, confidence, and ambitions? Where would we be if we had listened to those who were just trying to be helpful when they said:

- The world is flat; if you sail too far you will fall off!
- Electricity is a nice novelty, but it can't do anything meaningful!
- It is the year 1920; everything important has already been invented!
- You can't go faster than the speed of sound!
- You will never get a cell phone to work with anything smaller than a car battery!

Apparently, the people who invented or discovered the above items did not listen to their critics. Why should you continue to listen to your critics? If you stop listening to others and stop concentrating on all of the risks, you will have a chance to do better, be better, and get a lot more out of life for you and your family!

Start Doing the Right Things

What are some of the things you can do to help move you forward? Think about what you might need, and write a list of things you can do to move your goals forward. Research how to do what you want and the steps you will need to take. Think about whether some of the things should be done before others—these are the items that are more urgent. Think about the items that are more important than the others. Without getting too much into the details of some of the time management and prioritizing systems I have learned, if you do the following, you will be a long way there to doing what you should do when you should do it.

List what you need to do on any given day or week. The items that are more important and more urgent are the ones you should work on daily. The items that are more important but not urgent, you should work on when you can but on a regular basis (once a week, once a month, etc.).

Set your daily, weekly, and/or monthly goals as detailed as you feel will work for you. As you get some done, you will not only be making progress but you should feel awesome about the fact that you made them happen.

As you continue to make some progress, remember to take time to "sharpen the saw." I have heard different versions of this story of a man cutting wood with either a saw or axe but not making much progress as he struggles and sweats. Someone passes by, sees his slow progress, and asks, "When is the last time you sharpened that thing?" The man replies, "I don't have time for that. I have all this wood to cut."

Sharpening the saw for you might be taking a break, learning a new way to do something, or getting a good night's rest. In any event, the concept is that you can't always be in production mode. Sometimes you have to focus on production capacity. This is exactly the type of item that falls into that important but not urgent category and if ignored too long can affect your ability to do the daily or weekly important and urgent items.

One of the pieces of advice I have in achieving some success is: "Do the hardest thing first." While it is often a lot easier to be motivated to "pick the low-hanging fruit," it is easy to keep putting off the difficult items to the point where they never get done or don't get done at the right time to have the best overall impact.

What Will You Do and When?

A tool I use to keep on track with what I should be doing is a list of things I want to get done in the near future with some hopeful completion dates.

The following shows an actual draft of one of my goal lists for three areas I was working while writing this book:

Goals—9/25 work 20 hours per week	
The Better Men Group	
Test TBMGma@gmail.com	9/25
Send another 5 HF managers emails	9/25
Hedge Fund managers target list—cont. (5)	9/25
Draft and send New Profit help req em	9/29
Research 5 CEOs to send	10/2
Send 5 CEOs	10/3
Send another 5 HFM emails	10/10
Contact 2 other groups for advice	10/11
Send to 2 foundations	10/12
Draft logos; consider 1 page start up website	10/15
Add doing better by role courses	
Doing Better Book	
(incl stop doing negatives/sharpen the saw)	
Buy/read total of 15 books on doing better	12/31
Highlight balance of 400 be better book	9/26
Chapter draft and outline 15 hrs/wk	9/6 to 12/31
Add book notes to book ideas (2nd pass)	
Work on book outline	
Chapters 3–15 outline	9/28

Honored Memories	
Mark	
Research and target list photographers	9/28
Research LLC	10/3
Draft Wanderer ad	10/3
Contact planners/venues start	10/15
Evelyn_	
Order HM portfolio album	9/25
Assemble portfolio album	10/21

I didn't have a rigid schedule on when I updated this, but usually it was about every two weeks. It shows three separate long-term goals on which I am currently working:

- My dream to found and get funding for a new nonprofit corporation that I hope will do a tremendous amount of good.
- Helping my wife realize some success with her awesome artistic talents by creating custom wedding albums, memory boards, and other similar masterpieces.
- Getting this book written and published so that I can help you and others do a lot better in life while you help others and again do a tremendous amount of good.

I don't expect that too many extremely successful, otherwise driven, focused, fearless extra self-confident high achievers are going to read this book, nor would it help them much in reaching their goals. For the rest of us, lists, motivational quotes, reminders of why we are working so hard, and other tactics can make all the difference in the world in keeping us going.

What are the specific things that you are going to do, and when are you going to do them?

If you haven't done so yet, take out a piece of paper or pad, write your dream on it, put a time frame for when you want it, and list below it as many ideas as possible about how you can achieve your goal and specific things that you can do to make this happen.

Some of the things you might want to do include:

- Research online how to do what you want to have done, for example: "how to write a nonfiction book" or "how to start a small business" or how to just about anything. Find, save, and/or print articles, read, and learn.
- Find, buy, and read books on how to do what you are interested in doing. Many books are available online; buy used for a fraction of the cost.
- Search for small business and business-assistance publications and entities that support new ventures.

Write down your goal, a date you want to achieve it by, and interim goals with their own achievement dates. Keep track of your progress, and let your progress motivate you to keep going.

Your goal: _____

Achievement by target date: _____

Interim goals/milestones:

Milestone goal: _____ Date: _____

Milestone goal: _____ Date: _____

Milestone goal: _____ Date: _____

Behavior goals (daily, weekly, monthly):

Per day (hours, calls, words written, pages read, etc.)

Week ending: day/mo/yr   total:

Mon: Tue: Wed: Thu: Fri: Sat: Sun:

Week ending: day/mo/yr   total:

Mon: Tue: Wed: Thu: Fri: Sat: Sun:

Week ending: day/mo/yr   total:

Mon: Tue: Wed: Thu: Fri: Sat: Sun:

Week ending: day/mo/yr   total:

Mon: Tue: Wed: Thu: Fri: Sat: Sun:

Month Total:

Continue the list with weeks and months as needed or just weeks. This is what I do currently.

Is this something that you have to do to make progress toward your goal(s)? No. I am sure you can come up with something better, documenting your behavior goal targets and actual reached. You should probably set specific behavior goals within certain time frames and track your progress. Tools and habits like these are what keep us on track when the motivation to get something done now is not there. The other thing that helps us stay on track is the development of positive habits of getting things done. At the end of the day, in the week or the month when you have reached your behavior goals, you will have the satisfaction of knowing that you put in the work that you planned. You are moving yourself toward your goal. Again, you don't have to do any of this. You get to!

On a daily basis, first thing in the morning, you might want to develop a list of what you hope do get done that day. I find it extremely helpful. Spend at least a few minutes each morning listing the items you want to get done that day. Especially on busy days, it is liberating to get everything on paper in a list so I don't have to remember them all.

After you list all the items, you can either prioritize them by 1, 2, 3 or A, B, C, and/or set up time slots for each (8:00 a.m.–9:00 a.m. etc.). A daily planner book by month or weekly planner or monthly calendar with days on it can also help you to document appointments, deadlines, and other scheduled events. I use a two-page per day monthly planner into which I write my daily lists and future items. For longer-term items, I have a small monthly calendar section of the planner that I write in future appointments and meetings. Every now and then,

I get stressed when I know have to do something or be somewhere on a given day, as shown on my planner, but I can't read my own writing! Use lists, calendars, planners, sticky tabs, to-do lists, calendars on your phone, Outlook, tablet, laptop, or desktop notes, whatever works for you, but I recommend you try something so you can be more efficient, forget less, and be less stressed.

Chapter Summary

- Stop doing the wrong things.
- Start doing the right things.
- Set interim deadlines.
- Use tools to list your daily/weekly goals.
- Write things down and keep yourself on track.

Universal Truths

- "The world is your oyster [from whence your pearls will come]." —William Shakespeare.[11]
- Understand and you will conquer!
- The universe wants you to succeed!
- You can make things happen by acting yourself!
- The laws of nature are on your side!

There are some universal truths and laws of nature that can help explain how things work.

Work over Time Is Power!

I have heard it said it takes about three weeks to make a habit. I am not sure how accurate that statement is, but it definitely takes some time and repetition. When you are setting your daily and weekly behavior goals for what and how much you want to get done, put some thought into regular consistent patterns that can become habits. Maybe set aside Saturday mornings for two hours to work on one thing or weekday mornings or evenings to work on others.

Usually, for a day when I have a lot of things that I want to get done, I will write a list referring to my plan and adding in other things. As I am grinding out a larger project, I will mix in smaller items such as breaks. Case in point, after writing this book for a couple of hours on a weekend, I would take a break and mow the lawn, which takes an hour, and then come back and write some more. You might have more success blocking out larger blocks of time and staying focused on one thing.

There are some realities in this world that dictate how things work. For example, Newton's first law of physics is that a body at rest or at constant speed in a straight line will remain as is until acted on upon by a force. In other words, expect nothing to happen until you apply effort (force). Effort over distance is work. Work over time is power. The ability to do work is energy. Why is this important?

First, if you want something to happen, you have to put in work. Whatever your goal is, figure out the work you can to do achieve it and do it. You can research what needs to be done and plan what needs to be done forever, but nothing will happen until you do the work. If your goal is to build a house, you will want to have some drawings done defining the overall design, the features you want incorporated, and how the pieces and sections will fit together to make the whole. Until you or your builder does the work of building the foundation, walls, roof, and interior, you don't have a house, just a defined concept.

Second, "work over time is power" means that if you can do the work over time, you have the power to make things happen and change. This isn't just conjecture on my part or long-time accepted wisdom; it is grounded in the basic laws of physics and how the universe works. A house doesn't get built without construction work to make it happen. This book doesn't get written without writing work, and your goal doesn't get done without your work. This might seem like a harsh reality, but I see it as being a positive fact and opportunity: your work can make the changes you want happen! Again, it's not just me saying you can make things happen but a physical law of the universe! If you choose to make something happen and put in the work, it will happen!

While the ability to do work in the physical sense comes from limited resources (time, materials, money, etc.) the ability to do work in general comes from energy. Your own energy and desire to make things happen can be incredibly powerful in making things happen. If you desire it enough and have the energy, you can make it happen.

The awesome thing about the mental energy to make things happen is that it is within your control. Your energy comes from your attitude. You have control over your attitude. This means that you have the control to make things happen! Unlike the limits of the physical world, your mental energy, imagination, desire, and hope are renewable and as endless as you allow them to be. You can violate the laws of physics in essence by also having almost unlimited energy in the form of thought, heart, and optimism. Other energy without limits can be inspiration, motivation, creativity, willpower, happiness, and drive. With some of these energies, we let ourselves feel depleted and can't always seem to find them or at the right time. The great news though is that we have tools, tactics, and methods available to us to find, create, nurture, and grow these things if we choose to.

So, am I saying that we can create something from nothing? That we can make things from thoughts and change the world? Yes, you can initiate, inspire, motivate, and create. Then once you take action in the form of communication, deeds, and other actions, voila! Results and progress! That is part of the magic power that we have in this universe. We can create and make things happen by thinking about them and applying our force of action. If you wanted to, how many stories could you create and tell? How many different businesses could you create? With the spark of an idea, you can research, plan, then apply the work in the form of action, and you have the power to create your reality for your dreams, goals, and ambitions. You have that simple awesome power! How can you access it, use it, and make it work for you? The opportunities, possibilities, and potential for you to exercise your power to accomplish something are staggering and mind-boggling. You can let yourself be overwhelmed and crippled by that fact, or you can use it to fire your imagination, spark an idea, and give you something to focus your energy, work over time, power, and results!

Why Do People Act?

In whatever you want and whatever you do, you will be dealing with people. The better you do for or with them the more you will succeed. How do you know how you should treat people?

Most people have heard of The Golden Rule from the gospel story in the Bible. The current understood translation of The Golden Rule is "Do unto others as you would have them do unto you."

After multiple books, seminars, and experiences dealing with people, I thought, *We can do better*. So, I came up with The Platinum Rule: "Do unto others as they would have you do unto them." How do you know what they want done "unto them" or what will motivate them to act, decide, buy, agree, or otherwise partake in what you have to offer? It is hard enough to try to understand what one person wants or needs when they are right in front of you. How do you know what others want other than guessing?

As much as you might think you don't want to be, you are often in the role of a salesperson. In order to get people to do what you want, you need to communicate what it is you want and get them to agree to do it. You may be working on getting your child to do their homework or trying to negotiate a peace accord between two warring nations. In the end, you are selling a concept to people with wants and needs.

I have read books about selling, listened to audio programs, attended seminars, taken classes, and more importantly, spent years in direct sales of commercial building contracts of up to $5 million each. There are a lot of books about selling, the psychology of selling, why people buy, negotiation strategies, and dealing with people.

One of the first big enlightenments for me regarding selling was to learn the approach to concentrate not only on the features of what you are proposing or selling but also the benefits. This is significant because by considering and mentioning the benefits you are concentrating on the impact or potential impact on the person or people with whom you are dealing. In the case of getting your child to do their homework, you might say, "If you do your homework in the next hour, you don't have to clean your room tonight, and you will have time to watch TV." The feature in this case is not having to clean the room, and the benefit is to watch TV. If you are selling a car, the features might include antilock brakes and seat heaters. The benefits would be increased safety for the driver and passengers and more comfort, especially on those really cold winter days. It makes sense addressing the benefits, but what benefits do people really want and what really motivates people to act?

On one of the later selling techniques, I spent a fair amount of time training on had what I think was a good summary for why people act. Simply stated, the theory is that people act to attain either current or future pleasure or avoid current or future pain. Current or future pleasure in the car sale example might be, "You are going to be much more comfortable on the ride home with these seat heaters," or "Think of how smart you will feel about your investment when you trade in this car with its highest-in-industry future resale value." Current or future pain in the car sale example might be, "You can save the sting of costly repairs you will need on a used car with all new components" or "There is much less chance of skidding into a tree this winter with your antilock brakes."

In that later sales system, the understanding is that the most powerful motivating reason people act is to move away from current pain. If your sale or negotiation is face-to-face with one person or a group, you likely want to concentrate on asking questions that will give you insight into their current pains. You can then concentrate any proposed actions toward reducing their current pains. For the child reluctant to do homework, you might ask, "Is there a reason why you don't want to do your homework?"

The answer could be, "Because I don't know how do the math problems, and I feel stupid." You can then offer to look at the problems so the both of you can figure out how to do them.

In the case of two warring nations, you might ask each what their current worst problems are. One country might say that their people are starving because they have to devote all their resources toward defense of their country. When asked, "What about that really bothers you?" they might reveal the real pain, which is they feel trapped by the current situation and can't figure a way out. The other country might say their people are out of work because their farm-based economy is crippled by the war.

When asked what their biggest issue with that is, they might say they feel sick when they drive down streets and see so many jobless and homeless families. If they stop fighting, the first country could stop starving by refocusing their resources on food, and the second country could refocus their resources on rebuilding their farm-based economy. The second country would be back to work producing food. Would that all major conflicts have such complementary problem pains, but you get the point.

In real life, however, finding out what people's pains (or pleasures) are may not be that easy. First, when face-to-face with someone, they usually don't open up right away with what their real needs or wants are, let alone the reasons behind them. Usually, it is only after multiple questions. The problem is that people don't like to feel interrogated or grilled. At the beginning of a discussion, you can make this easier by saying something like, "Is it okay if I ask you some questions?" Hopefully the answer is yes. I have found it helpful to also say, "Bear with me if it sounds like am asking the same question in different ways at times. For me to best help you, I am trying to find out some of the whys behind your whats. Is that okay?" If you can, find the current or future pains and/or pleasure hopes they have; you can tailor what you can offer and be much more successful with your "sale" or negotiation.

Oftentimes, you can guess what might be pain or pleasure indicators, which can lead to discovering actual pains or pleasures. One of the other techniques from that training program was how to make questions seem less threatening by asking in the negative. For an in-person conversation in a car sale, you might ask, "I don't suppose you have ever considered future resale value in deciding which car to buy."

Possible answer: "Actually, that is a big factor for me."

A response: "You wouldn't want to tell me why?"

Answer: "Last time I traded in my car, I got almost nothing from the dealer." Maybe a simple "And?"

Then a response of, "I felt like I was being robbed. Afterward, I felt stupid for taking the deal!"

There is the pain! There is now a much better chance of making that sale, especially if you can get another feature-based pain or two.

What if you are dealing with multitudes of people to whom you cannot ask probing questions (or a lone person who will not answer any questions)? Let's assume you are the director of sales and marketing for child and teen clothing manufacturer trying to promote and create sales of a new line of winter coats. You are developing an advertising campaign. How might you tap into potential customers' pains or pleasures to help them buy?

For pains, you might concentrate on messages that include:

- Don't let your children suffer from this winter's biting cold.
- Will your kids be the only ones without these coats?
- Wouldn't you feel awful if your child got sick from not having the right coat?

For pleasures, you might use:

- Be the best parents ever!
- Show them you love them!
- Keep them warm and safe!

The theory I am trying to convey with these examples is that everyone acts for their own reasons. If someone does not have a reason to act, they likely won't. If you have a person or group who has no pain to avoid or pleasure to gain from what you are offering, find someone or a group who does.

The famous psychologist Abraham Maslow, in his 1943 paper "A Theory of Human Motivation," drafted his "The Hierarchy of Needs."[12] Within this hierarchy, he not only listed the five basics needs that people have but prioritized them.

1. Physiological—the basic needs for the body to survive, such as food, water, shelter, etc.
2. Safety—including physical, personal, financial, health, and well-being.
3. Love and belonging—the need for family, relationships, interpersonal bonds.

4. Esteem—self-confidence and respect from others.
5. Self-actualization—achieving your desires and goals and doing the best you can.

From Wikipedia, the full expanded version is:[13]

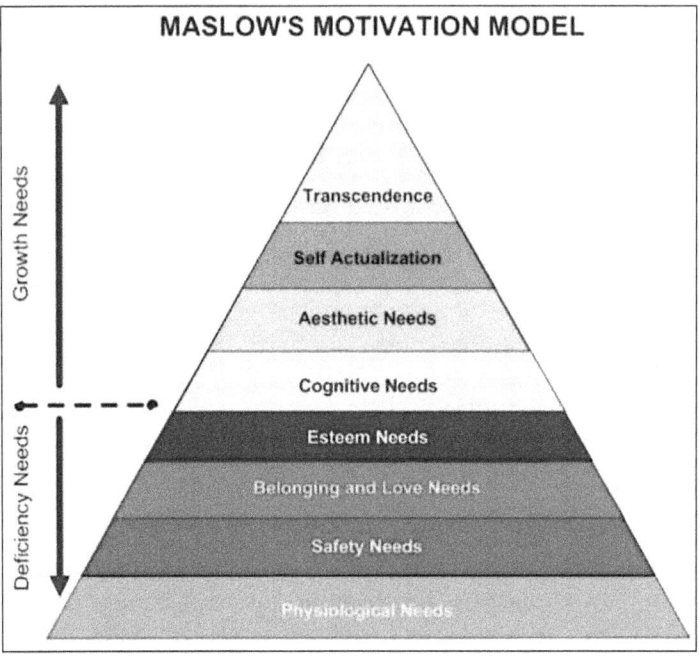

By better understanding the whys behind people's whats, we can help motivate them to act and best help them. The Maslow model shows the most important needs of physiological as the base or foundation for all the other needs. Let's face it, if you are starving or dying of thirst, you don't care as much about being respected and probably don't care if your shirt matches your pants. It gets a bit more complicated when you consider present needs versus future needs. The point here is that, again, you achieve your goals when you help others with goods and services. If you can't determine what peoples' specific wants and needs are individually, you can at least gain some insight into what they could be by understanding their general needs and offering to satisfy them.

The Business of Business Is People

As you continue to think about your goals and what you want, remember, as I stated earlier in the book, that we succeed by providing things that help or make people happy. The better you do at this the better you do overall. At his point in the book, I hope you are excited about working toward you goals and achieving them. The better you help people, the better you do overall. I also propose that you consider that "the business of business is people." That actually sounds like I heard it from someone else, but if so, I can't remember who.

Over the years, I have met people and learned from experience and books some ways to be more effective dealing with people. Some sales courses have said that you should focus on not only the features of what you are selling but also the benefits the features provide. Another sales and negotiating method said that you should ask questions to find out what "pains" or difficulties people have and tailor your products to meet their pains. The minimal personal coaching training I had helped to focus on what would work best for each individual.

Back to The Platinum Rule mentioned earlier in the book. Unless you know how someone wants to be treated or what they need, how can you help?

What if you see someone on the side of a busy street late at night and it is raining. Do you offer them a ride? If they say no, do you just drive on? What if that person is looking for their child who wandered off from the car a ways ahead?

How about if are trying to sell a couple a house and spend most of your time talking about how close it is to a beach where the kids can go swimming. You then find out that last year they had a child who drowned at a different beach and never want to be near a beach again.

What I am getting at is we can do better. Maybe we do not assume what is important to you is important to others. You wouldn't paint someone's house your favorite color, unless it was the color they happened to want. Someone isn't going to buy your truck if what they only want is a bicycle.

It can be frustrating at times figuring out what people really want. You can ask them, they can tell you, but unless you understand why they want something you might not really be able to help them. For example, say you work at a hardware store and someone comes in looking for a circular saw. You ask them what they plan to use it for, and they say to cut plywood and two-by-fours. Makes sense that should work. You ask them, "If you don't mind saying, what are you building?" They tell you a gazebo. You say, "Oh, great, is it going to be like an octagon or round?"

They say round, and you ask, "Have you thought about how you are going to make the curved cuts?"

They say, "Well, no, not really."

You say suggest a saber saw (or other saw to cut curves). More than likely they ask, " Where can I find a saber saw?"

You just made an extra sale.

In order to get anyone to do what you want (in the case above, buy tools), you need to know what they want. What motivates them. What is their *why*? A term I picked up from Logan Stout's *Grit Factor*. Conversely, what is their *why not*? If you want good service from someone, you might not want to say insulting comments, be disrespectful, talk angrily, or shout. Keep in mind they, too, have a perspective and paradigm forming in their head based on what they're hearing from you. If you need help, do you want them to think, *What a shame, that poor person really needs some help*. Or how about if they think, *What an arrogant jerk. At best I will do nothing, but maybe I will try to make it worse*. Which situation do you think will work out better for you?

One of the easiest things to do to do better in almost any relationship, business or personal, is to be a good listener. A lot of people like to hear themselves talk and often don't listen to others, especially if they have a different point of view. Again, the business of business is people. How do you interact with people? You do so by communicating—giving information and receiving information.

If you spend most of your time doing all the talking, what are you really trying to accomplish? Are you trying to make yourself sound smart, wise, funny, or important? If so, then why? If you hope to find out more about the other person and what they want, some well-phrased questions and a lot of listening will get you a long way toward understanding them. You are also bound to have people value what you say more when you finally have something to say if it is related to what they said. The is an old adage: "Still waters run deep." I also remember the term "babbling brook" for noisy, shallow, fast-running waters.

Keep in mind, a large portion of our communication is nonverbal. I looked it up online and found at least two sources that say that 55 percent or so of face-to-face communication is by things other than words, including eye contact, posture, arm position, hand gestures, tone, volume, and others such as facial expressions, sighs, etc. I remember years ago in my search to become better in sales I read *How to Read a Person Like a Book* by Gerard Nierenberg. You can tell a lot about someone based on their posture, tone, and facial expressions. Good poker players use these signs to get a handle on the strength of other players cards.

Some of what I remember includes how folded arms often indicate a guarded, self-protective mindset, and speaking fast can indicate excitement. I also remember reading that the FBI, while questioning, can tell if someone is lying or not by where their eyes are looking. From what I recall in rough terms, if you ask someone a question and their eyes look to the left, they are trying to recall the factual information before they answer and are likely telling the truth. If they look to the right, they are formulating a response from made-up thoughts and are not telling the truth. There a lot of nuances that affect the impression, including looking left low, left high, right low, right high, but you get the general idea.

Why does this even matter? Again, the business of business is people. We interact with people by communicating. You have more control over your communications than just what you say. Yes, words count, but how they are said, and what you are doing while you say them can be arguably more important. Wouldn't you like to know if while you are talking with people whether they are lying to you or telling the truth? How do you think people react to you when you look angry? How about when you smile? How do you react to others when they shout or look angry? Keep in mind, people remember how you make them feel. How do you feel after someone snaps or yells at you?

While we are on the topic of communication, I want to share with you a tactic for dispute and argument diffusion and resolution I learned from a marriage counselor when my wife and I had a rough patch.

First, have the offended person state what their problem or grievance is while you listen, without frustrated sighs, rolling your eyes, or other. Then restate what they said calmly: "So, from what I understand, you have a problem with my …" Then verify with "is that right?" If you are corrected, restate and ask again, "Is that right?" Once you have it right, ask, "Anything else?"

If your intent is to correct something that you did, you should at least know and acknowledge what you did wrong. In any event, showing interest in understanding the problem and listening go a long way to diffusing a tense situation. By helping to set the tone of the conversation at a reasonable and productive level, you also have a much better chance of resolution. Keep in mind the other person may be fired up and ready to be combative. If you find yourself getting combative, think hard about whether you really want to resolve your conflict or if you want to win the argument.

Chapter Summary

- Work over time is power.
- You have to give to get.
- The business of business is people.
- People act because of their needs and interests, not yours.
- Communication is much more than words only.

Do Better by Choice

- You have the magic power of choice!
- There but for my choices go I!
- Choose your path; choose your destiny!
- Choose to be successful and it will happen!
- If you choose not to decide, you still have made a choice!

We have the awesome power of free will and choice every minute of every day to decide what we want, how we react to things, whether to try something, and many other choices from the mundane to the sublime. From what to have for breakfast to taking steps to reduce world hunger, you can choose what you want to do. From your attitude in the morning to your actions all day, you get to choose to how you get to consider all of your choices available to you, burdens and responsibilities or empowering freedom and exciting opportunities!

I saw a recent TV commercial that said that we make thirty-five thousand choices per day, a fact confirmed by a recent Google search. To me that feels overwhelming to try to get a handle on, so I choose to concentrate on identifying the choices I can make to do better and be better and let the others proceed as they will.

One of the five items at the beginning of this section is a statement that I heard or read somewhere, and it really strikes home for me on the impact of my choices: "There but for my choices go I." This is a modification of the statement by John Bradford, a sixteenth-century preacher paraphrasing a section of the Bible: "There but for the grace of God go I." There is wisdom in both. The first shows how much power we have over own situations by the choices we make. The second is more about how much of our lives is outside of our control.

In this section of the book, I want to share with you some thoughts, insights, and wisdom about how you can do better and be better by making better choices and decisions. I understand that a choice may not strictly be the same thing as a decision, but bear with me as I use the words interchangeably to describe our power over our lives with them. I don't think it matters much in the long run if that is because I choose to use the two terms the same or if it is because I decide to.

In most of the free world, you can choose your career, your spouse, where you want to live, how you want to live, where to go for vacation, what to say publicly, and many other aspects of your life. You can choose what you want to eat, when, and where.

Some of the more powerful choices we have include choosing whether your life has meaning, your dreams and goals, and choosing to be happy. Some choices and decisions are complex; some are simple. Some are easy; some are hard. Some things are thrust upon you not by your choice, but how you react to them is your choice.

We have a tendency to fall into patterns and habits that keep us from easily changing our behaviors, but again, we can choose to overcome and improve. We get to choose to seek help, to help others, and how we react to our setbacks and accomplishments.

Some of the more complex decisions we have to make can include multiple factors for us to consider, short-term and long-term consequences, the different people affected, and varying levels of risk. There are many tools that you can use to help you with complex decision-making and choice, which you can find out more about online and use, including:

- List pros and cons.
- Create a decision matrix.
- Consider the consequences.
- Ask others and weigh their opinions.

- Decide by committee vote.
- Ask yourself, "Choose this to what end?"
- You can delegate and let someone else decide.
- Some people use, "What would Jesus do?"
- Use your intuition and "go with your gut."
- Delay deciding until it does not matter anymore.
- Choose based on what meets your values.
- Think about the impacts of not choosing at all.
- List what is in your best interest.
- List what is in the best interest of others.
- Consider effects on your short- or long-term goals.

You could also use the tool shown in the movie *Office Space*, which is like a checkerboard mat with different suggestions like, yes, no, move forward, etc. with which you can physically "jump to a conclusion." I would not necessarily recommend this for the more important choices you consider.

We have choices we make daily that affect our lives and can affect the lives of others. How do you speak with the people with whom you interact? How do you react to how or what others say to you? Whole books, courses, and studies deal with different ways to make better choices and decisions. How can we make the best choices to enable us to do better and be better?

Sometimes it may be counterintuitive what the best choice may be. If we want long-term freedom to live with the best options available, we may want to conform to others' norms to stay in school, work hard, put in years of hard work, and eventually have more freedom. We can struggle at times with instant gratification versus long-term rewards. While it is great that we have so much freedom to choose, we have to be careful not to forget that, for good or for bad, our choices have consequences.

In order to make an informed decision, you may need to do extensive research and solicit the advice of experts. Even then, you may need to rely on your common sense, intuition, or some combination of those along with the data and advice you have collected. For some complex important decisions, you can do as much research and solicit advice, but you need to trust your gut.

About ten years ago I had a scare where I thought I was having a stroke. I had difficulty putting concepts into words and remembering simple things like my home phone number. After going to the emergency room and having a CAT scan, they determined that I was likely having a transient ischemic attack (TIA) or mini-stroke from restricted blood flow. Their suggestion was to put me on a daily aspirin regimen to thin my blood and make the blood flow easier. This has pretty much worked to date with some occasional TIA vision blurring and occasional ear ringing or tinnitus. On the fringe of the CAT scan films, they did notice a lump in my throat and recommended that I follow up with a throat specialist.

My primary care doctor referred me to a well-known local specialist who did an ultrasound test and recommended a relatively simple needle biopsy to which I agreed. She said the office would review and make an appointment with me to discuss the results and her recommendations. I met with her, and she told me that the results of the biopsy was that I had a nodule from which the few cells they collected were "suspicious for being cancerous." She recommended that I have a procedure done to remove that half of my thyroid, and while still on the surgery table they would do a more detailed pathology study of the removed half thyroid. If it showed cancer, then they would remove the balance of my thyroid. Wait, WHAT?

I was not exactly sure what my thyroid did for me other than being some sort of gland that some overweight people have problems with. I was sure that I was not comfortable with losing half of it on a "suspicious" or maybe. I had heard of some new advances in molecular profiling of different tissues and cancers to better diagnose and treat cancers and wanted to know more. I also wanted to get another opinion.

After discussing my thyroid situation with a doctor I know, he did some research and gave me a printed set of protocols by The American Thyroid Association for addressing thyroid "nodules" or lumps from one to two centimeters in size. The decision matrix flow chart and narrative actually concurred with what was proposed for me with removing half of the thyroid based on a "suspicious" pathology report determination and proceeding with testing that half while the patient was still on the table to decide whether to remove the balance. I was not convinced that it made sense for me and still wanted another opinion.

I sought out and met with another thyroid specialist affiliated with a larger hospital. He was an older gentleman who reviewed my scan and biopsy results, dismissed my questions about molecular profiling, and concurred with the approach to cut my throat and see. I was unimpressed and still far from convinced. Do I choose to have the procedure done, find another doctor, or do nothing?

After some consideration, I decided to reach out to the doctor who had treated both my wife and me years ago, explain my concerns, and ask for a referral of a good doctor for me. He was now a world-renowned specialist at a prestigious institution, and I hoped he could help. Through his office he said that he remembered me, had a doctor recommendation, and wished me the best of luck. I was able to get an appointment soon and met with him to discuss my concerns and options.

He was a soft-spoken older gentleman with an air of confidence. He reviewed my scan and biopsy results and recommended that they do a new biopsy for themselves. He also answered some of my questions about molecular profiling. He said they could do that there but it might not be worth the effort, depending on what the biopsy showed. I remember feeling a little frustrated about having to wait again for a test and results, but when I asked when we could do the procedure and get results, he said we could do the biopsy now, hang around for a couple of hours, and then discuss his findings and recommendations. I thought that was great, so we went forward with the biopsy.

I had my dad with me for support. After lunch at the cafeteria, we went back to see the doctor again. He said that he did not believe that the cells looked suspicious for cancer and that he recommended that we follow up with an ultrasound in six months. If there was no change, then I should follow up again in a year. Part of me felt exonerated, and part of me felt like maybe I should just keep going until I heard what I wanted. I did feel better when I told my primary care doctor about the specialist I saw and what he said. He was amazed that I was able to get in to see that specialist since even the doctors have a tough time getting to see him for themselves.

It has been about ten years now with no change in the nodule size after checking with ultrasounds after the first six months, then a year, then a few years. The standard protocol to cut out half the thyroid, on a maybe might work for most but not for me. This wasn't my first medical issue, and it was my choice, my decision to find out more. It ended up saving at least half of my thyroid if not the entire thing. Live and learn. Is it just me, or does thyroid medicine sound like a real cutthroat business?

When we make bad decisions or see others make bad decisions, hopefully we learn from them and don't repeat them. The first part of any journey, goal, or even our day starts with choosing where we want to go, what we want, or what to wear. If we put in the effort to research and consider the consequences of our major decisions, we cannot fault ourselves if things go wrong.

We make so many choices and decisions that affect our lives and the lives of others, and our choices have consequences. The importance of some choices is apparent, like whether to get married or whether to go forward with a medical procedure. Others may not be so obvious, such as deciding to have another couple of drinks before driving, overeating to the point of dangerous obesity, or procrastinating doing things to move your goals forward. A big part of doing better and being better is the choices you make. It is an awesome responsibility and gives you tremendous power! Will you choose the blue pill and remain Mr. Anderson or choose the red pill and become "The One?"

Always keep in mind, your choices have consequences. I saw a quote the other day that said that your choice of your spouse or long-term partner will determine 90 percent or more of your overall happiness or misery in life. While I still believe that happiness is a personal choice, I agree that your earlier choices make your future choices easier or harder at times. For instance, it is much easier to decide to eat a healthy meal if you choose to buy only healthy food when you go shopping. Choose to own the consequences of your decisions, learn to make better choices from the bad ones, and revel in rewards of the good choices you have made.

In doing some research on choices and decisions, I found some wise quotes from others that stood out:

1. "In the end, we only regret the chances we didn't take and the decisions we didn't make." —Anonymous
2. "The most difficult thing is the decision to act, the rest is mere tenacity. The fears are paper tigers. You can do anything you decide to do. You can act to change and control your life, and the procedure, the process is its own reward." —Amelia Earhart[14]
3. "Good decisions come from experience and experience comes from bad decisions." —Anonymous (Although I would add that experience can also come from learning about others, their decisions, choices, and impacts.)
4. "You always do what you want to do. This is true with every act. You may say that you had to do something, or that you were forced to, but actually whatever you do, you do by choice. Only you have the power to choose for yourself." —W. Clement Stone[15]
5. "Every positive change in your life begins with a clear, unequivocal decision to either do something or stop doing something." —Anonymous

We make choices and decisions daily, some more important than others. Some of which we can predict the outcome from such as whether to get up out of bed, go to work, and keep your job and have the income to feed yourself and your family. Other choices we make might not be so easy to predict the impact from such as driving too fast, investing time or money into a new venture, or deciding whether to take any of the risks associate with potential choices. You might look at decisions from a risk versus benefit view. My wife reminded me recently of something I said years ago that she still thinks about: "Never risk more that you are willing to lose." I don't remember who originally said that to me, but I try to keep that in mind when making small and large choices and trying not to make really bad ones.

How do you assess whether a choice will be good or bad? I challenge you to consider what bad or good means to you. Will it fall within or violate your basic values? What are the short-term and long-term consequences? What other impacts might that choice have on you or others? How important are those impacts to you? It may sound hard or complicated, but with the awesome power of free will and choice comes the great responsibility of choosing what you do. As with other aspects of life, you are not the only one to ever face a similar situation. You can learn about how others have done in your situation and ask them for advice on how you might best proceed.

Think of all the wonderful choices we have and the control that gives us over our own destiny! From whether to hit the snooze button on the alarm to what dreams and goals to pursue, we control our days and many aspects of our lives. We have so much access to information to help us with decisions and choices. You can choose to complain about things outside of your control and blame others for your lack of success or decide to own your destiny, choose a dream, make it happen, and enjoy the ride!

Chapter Summary

- You have the awesome power of free will!
- Your choices and decisions make your destiny!
- Learn from your previous choices and decisions.
- Learn from others' choices and decisions and do better.
- Choose your dreams and decide to be successful!

Dealing Better with Crises

- "That which does not kill us makes us stronger!"—Friedrich Nietzsche[16]
- You are stronger than you think!
- No one is an island—you are not alone!
- Others have been through similar trials!
- Hope is free!

How stable is your life and your ability to work, excel, and reach your goals or even get by? What happens when life gets in the way as it inevitably does? How are you going to deal with a life-changing crisis like being diagnosed with cancer, life-threatening injuries from a car accident, the death of a family member, the loss of a home to a catastrophe, or other crises?

Dealing with any of the above crises or other crises is a lot easier when you have a stable foundation of otherwise good health, financial stability, and a network of family and friends that you have been able to maintain by keeping balance in your life. Even with the best support structure you will inevitably face some important difficulties with crises in your life.

Some Firsthand Experience with Crises

If there is anything in this book about which I am qualified to offer some helpful advice and tactics to cope, it is the subject of life crises. At age twenty-five, living in greater Denver, two thousand miles from my home, I was in a car accident in which I broke five ribs. I have been in pain before, but when the x-ray tech told me to turn on my right side for better x-ray images, I tried, couldn't, sat up, and my body shook uncontrollably. It hurt a lot! After a few days, the pain was a lot less, but I was still trying not to sneeze for six months!

A couple of months prior to the accident, I had been going to optometrists for glasses because my vision seemed off. I had some mild double vision and was prescribed some glasses with prism lenses to help try to fix the problem. At a cookout, friends had invited a medical student who for some reason I can't remember was checking different people's pupil responses to light. When he checked my pupils, he noticed that they did not contract or dilate with the shining and removing of light to them. It seemed strange but no big deal.

A couple of weeks after the accident, I mentioned some of the vision symptoms I was having and some numbness I had in my arm to a doctor following up on my accident injuries. He suggested that I see a neurosurgeon. I saw the neurosurgeon, and he ordered an MRI. I still remember to this day. I was living two thousand miles from home, alone in an apartment, and got the call at 6:00 p.m. on a Friday. He told me that I had a brain tumor that was inoperable and that maybe radiation could be used to treat it.

I don't remember much of the next couple of days. I just stayed in watching some TV and processing (we didn't have any internet back in 1992). By Sunday evening, I had come to grips with the fact that the brain tumor was either going to kill me, disable me, or I would be fine. I called a friend of mine, and we talked briefly. I then called my parents, who I usually called every Sunday anyway. After a brief discussion, I agreed to come back home and let them help me with getting treated and dealing with the brain tumor. It actually didn't hit me that hard.

You see, I was just twenty-five years old. I was not married, no children, and no one depending on me. The most difficult thing for me was the impact I knew my crisis was going to have on my parents and siblings. I had a local girlfriend I had met on a recent vacation back home who was wonderful to me through my brain tumor ordeal, even though long term we were not meant for each other. I also had the luxury of a core supportive family to help me. It was humbling to realize I could use the help and that I wasn't the know-everything self-reliant person I thought I was. It did make it easier to accept the help, realizing that my parents wouldn't have it any other way to help however they could. No parent wants to outlive their child, and we had always been close.

I was successfully cured with five weeks of radiation. No sign of the cancer. It should be gone forever! Living back in New England, up in Maine and feeling lucky to be alive, I wanted to do something to help others. After volunteering for a few events and patient visits through the American Cancer Society, they put me in touch with a woman who had also survived a brain tumor and wanted to start a support group for others.

We started the group for patients and family members, starting with a handful of us meeting twice a month, once a month for shared experience and self-help, and once a month with a guest speaker (neurosurgeon, radiation oncologist, social worker, etc.). In an attempt to reach more people, I worked with the local TV stations to develop and run some public service announcements (PSAs) about our group. A special young single mom of two boys and survivor of a brain tumor saw one of the PSAs, had a friend call, and attended a support group meeting. Evelyn and I are a match made in heaven. After a couple of meetings with her, I asked her to meet me for coffee under the guise of talking about how we could build the support group. Plans changed to dinner. Dinner went awesome. A year and a half later we were married, and two months ago we celebrated our twenty-fifth wedding anniversary. A year or so after we got married, Evelyn's boss where she used to work making sandwiches, reminded her that when she was working and saw the PSA she had said, "I am going to marry that man" when she saw me on the TV screen. I never stood a chance. Evelyn is my muse and the best thing that has ever happened to me.

About six months after Evelyn and I started seeing each other, she started having headaches and other symptoms again. A piece left over from her brain tumor was growing again and in an inoperable location. Unlike my tumor, the type she had was not very receptive to radiation treatment.

This time, I really cared about the outcome and wanted to do everything I could to help. It was 1995, with no internet to speak of, but I was lucky we lived not far from the University of New England, a medical school with great medical library resources. Off I would go with my medical dictionary and notebook.

I spent a lot of nights there researching and reviewing information from Evelyn's medical records. I found out that in her postsurgical report it was recommended that she have a focused radiation beam procedure called radiosurgery for the remnant piece of tumor that could not be safely taken out, which was now growing. Worse than that, it became clear that Evelyn suffered a lot of pain and some long-term damage from not having the tumor originally diagnosed until over a year after the symptoms started.

There was a clear recommendation on her initial MRI report saying that while nothing was seen that a follow-up MRI with contrast should be done. That did not happen until another year and a half later of pain, loss of hearing in one ear, facial nerve paralysis, and eye misalignment. When the MRI with contrast was done it showed a large bright spot, indicating a tumor larger than a golf ball.

We had a decision to make. Pursue payback and compensation for the egregious medical incompetence and sue her doctor up against a statute of limitations running out, or focus solely on getting her treated and getting better. We decided on the latter, and I am glad to this day that we did.

Why all this background? Along with the hundreds of patients and family members I have met who were facing brain tumors and/or cancer diagnoses, I have my own personal experience both as a patient and as a support person. So, as you read the following insights into and suggestions for coping with crises, you have some idea of the personal reality and pain that went into this knowledge and wisdom with the hope that it will help you.

Tools and Tactics for Dealing Better with Crises

First of all, there is no "I don't know if I can handle this." You will handle it no matter how bad it gets. You have no choice but to handle whatever comes your way. So, take that potential stress right out of your fear and worry list. You will, however, deal with what is coming either well or poorly. The good news is you get to choose how. We all have to come to grips with the grief associated with bad news, impending potential loss, or coping with a loss. Your situation might be unique, but many people have faced similar situations, and you can gain insight into your own trials by learning from theirs.

The commonly accepted five stages of grief are as follows:

1. shock and/or denial
2. anger
3. bargaining
4. depression
5. acceptance

While I agree that the preceding five stages of grief are common for most people, I challenge whether anger and depression are always to be a significant part of the process, or even a necessary step for everyone. Personally, I try to minimize both anger and depression but understand they can happen naturally. The concern is the negative impact that anger and depression can have on personal motivation to continue and the attitude of the support people around you.

It does help to understand that it is widely believed that anger comes from fear and/or pain. It is a natural emotion that can help motivate taking action during crises. The danger with being angry is that it can cloud your judgment and make you more likely to make rash not-well-thought-out decisions. Prolonged anger can also rob you of joy, happiness, and relationships with others. Personally, I believe the opposite of happiness is not sadness; it is anger.

Depression, in the case of crises, can be feeling sad, anxious, numb, or hopeless. While it can be a natural reaction to feel these things short term, if you let them grow too much, they can cripple your ability to move forward and do what you need to do to make things better.

Below are some tools to help you get out of the depression phase, move past the acceptance phase, and start dealing with the crisis and make things better.

I have found that the following ten things that can drastically improve your handling of difficult crises:

1. Identify a hopeful outcome.
2. List steps or tasks to give that outcome the best chance.
3. Solicit help to achieve that outcome and build a team.
4. Consider appointing a point person to coordinate things like medical tests, scans, doctor appointments, treatments, etc.
5. Either you or someone you trust should research your situation and things that can affect outcomes.
6. Research and reach out to others and organizations who have dealt with similar crises.
7. Use tools like writing in a journal or using humor to keep spirits up.
8. Have someone and/or you yourself check records, paperwork, and follow up as needed.
9. Cut yourself some slack if you feel down or stressed at times.
10. Maintain hope and maximize quality of life whenever possible!

1. Identify a hopeful outcome.

Again, like any other goal, identify what you want to happen. The outcome may not be in your total control, but having something to work for gives you some control over what will happen. With Evelyn, at the time of her recurrence, my goal was to do everything I could to get her cured with the minimal amount of her pain and suffering. In her case, we did pretty well.

2. List steps or tasks to give that outcome the best chance.

For me, with Evelyn, I would go after dinner to the medical library and research the specific tumor, treatment options, and outcomes. It was all new doctor-speak medical language, but with the help of a medical dictionary I was able to get by.

I also collected as many of the medical records and past MRI films as possible to be ready for the team of doctors we would contact.

3.   Solicit help to achieve that outcome and build a team.

Since the procedure that looked like the best hope was not available locally, we decided to go back to the large teaching hospital in Boston, where I had been treated. The doctor who had treated me was all over the medical literature as a specialist in the type of treatment that looked like Evelyn's best hope: radiosurgery or focused high-single-dose radiation.

I also found it more comfortable contacting the Brain Tumor Clinic nurses and staff that I already knew from my stint there. People are often more willing to help a recognized person, especially from a previous positive experience, and they were great to us.

4.   Consider appointing a point person to coordinate things like medical tests, scans, doctor appointments, treatments, etc.

For Evelyn, she had me to help coordinate things. I was glad to, and it helped me to feel like I was doing something to help. She had enough to deal with. For me, it was my dad. He made all kinds of things happen in a short time frame. It was humbling for me to go home and get help from my parents at twenty-five years old, but I am glad I decided to. If I had procrastinated and not addressed my situation, it likely would have killed me.

5.   Either you or have someone you trust should research your situation and things that can affect outcomes.

Again, for Evelyn, I researched the different treatments and options. There were some aspects of the different methods for the treatment we were considering. One of the radiation doctors who had spoken at our group put me in touch with the hospital's staff physicist who explained the different methods and their effects in lay terms that I could understand. As it turned out, he taught classes to medical students on the subject.

When it came to our decision on where to have Evelyn's treatment done, it came down to who would be using the tools versus what tools would they be using.

6. Research and reach out to others and organizations who have dealt with similar crises.

I reached out to different national associations and foundations and collected literature on brain tumors in general, Evelyn's specific tumor, treatments, etc. Many of the pamphlets and contacts we had already collected for our support group meetings. My cofounder of the group also had a similar treatment for a similar type of tumor and was a great resource both for Evelyn and me.

7. Use tools like writing in a journal or using humor to keep spirits up.

For me it was easy to keep a sense of humor and my spirits if not up then at least not down. Part of me was on autopilot going through the motions. With Evelyn, I kept my sense of humor and helped her with her spirits when I could. She did some writing in a journal, and our support group meetings helped.

8. Have someone and/or you yourself check records, paperwork, and follow up as needed.

If Evelyn had someone checking her records for her first brain tumor, she would have been diagnosed much sooner. When I checked her post-surgical records and learned of the recommended follow-up treatment that was never pursued, we stopped seeing the doctor who missed that. My dad noticed the fact in my records that my radiation treatment was supposed to be for five weeks, not six weeks, as the technicians thought. I was saved a week of arguably the portion of radiation with the highest chance of unwanted side effects.

Keep in mind, no one is perfect. Things get missed all the time. Even the best professionals and their staff miss things sometimes. It will never be as important to them as it is to you. You have more time and energy to devote to double-checking records and recommendations for consistency and accuracy. Do not let anyone intimidate you into thinking you can't understand basic communication and follow up.

9.   Cut yourself some slack if you feel down or stressed at times.

It is understandable to feel down sometimes, frustrated, beaten down, and upset. I believe, in many cases, it is more difficult for the family members and friends of someone facing a difficult crisis than it is for the one facing it. For many worst-case outcomes, the person with the crisis will not survive and have to deal with the aftermath. The burden in that case will fall on those who are left behind. Also, everyone understands if the afflicted person feels down, but the caregivers and support people are expected to stay positive. Take some breaks as needed and recharge when you can.

As a support person, you will likely feel at times like you wish you could do more to help. Take it from me who has seen a fair amount of people with no one there for them. If you are there and support where you can, you can do almost no wrong!

10.   Maintain hope and maximize quality of life whenever possible.

One of my biggest fears in starting a support group for brain tumor patients, family members, and support people is that we would all get together, talk about our tough situations and concerns, and all end up feeling miserable and hopeless by the end of meeting.

My fear did not come to be a reality. We did not get into a whiny self-pity party; we talked more about technical things dealing with treatments and coping than feelings. At the end of each meeting though, I did have us go around the room and have each of us say something positive or something we are looking forward to. The only person who had a difficult time with that was a brain tumor patient who was also a psychologist and practicing therapist. Go figure!

Crisis and Opportunity

There is a school of thought that says with every crisis comes an opportunity. In any event, you can at least gain a new perspective. Other things seem less important or petty. You tend to focus more on things with higher priorities. At times it can be liberating. While I am not necessarily a big country music fan, I do really like the hit from a few years ago by Tim McGraw "Live Like You Were Dying." The song refers to a relatively young man being diagnosed with a difficult illness, and how he deals with that fact strikes home to me as a brain cancer survivor.

When you are facing your next crisis, keep in mind the following: your attitude will have an effect on your outcome. As an extreme example, if you are too depressed to eat, go see a doctor or get treatment. You will not do well. Your attitude is also contagious and affects the people around you. With a negative attitude, you find that people want to spend less time with you partly because it is so emotionally draining for them to do so. No matter how much or how often you want to do so, do everything you can to stop feeling like and playing the victim role. You have the opportunity in a crisis to be a hero! In most cases, to be or at least look like a hero is to go along with the flow, do what needs to be done, not complain, make a positive statement once in a while, and smile sometimes!

In my case, facing potential death in the near future was pretty easy for me to deal with at age twenty-five without anyone depending on me. Just before being diagnosed with my brain cancer, I was arrogant, narcissistic, self-centered, and knew everything. While it took me meeting my now wife, Evelyn, for me to become a much better person, being told of my diagnosis was immediately humbling. I didn't do much but go through all the scans, appointments, and radiation treatments. I was taken aback some a few weeks after going through the process when my mom said that I was her hero for how I coped with my health crisis. To this day, I don't think I was much of a hero. If anything, the support both of my parents gave me made them the heroes. I did not actually do anything resembling heroic until Evelyn's tumor started growing again. At that point, I did step up and believe I was very helpful.

It has been said that hardship can either grind you down or grind you to a polish. Don't let the grind tear away who you are. Instead, let the grind tear away the superficial layers that are holding you back. When facing difficult crises, people often find their best selves. It seems a lot less important to hold some petty or even big grudge when someone is dying. Forgiveness seems to come a little easier. You have amazing strength within you to deal with anything that comes your way, even the worst crisis.

As a support person in a crisis, you have the opportunity to shine, to be of great value, to be a big help, to be a hero. Simple support, being there, and offering help when you can are heroic and difficult at times. You might fear doing or saying the wrong thing, but you push past your fear and do what you can to help. Bravery is not the absence of fear; it is acting in spite of it.

Again, with crises can come opportunities. Opportunities that can arise from natural disasters include a sense of community when we step up and help each other through such difficulties. We learn how to better barricade and design buildings for floods and hurricanes, engineer structures to withstand earthquakes, stock up for longer-term shutdowns, and develop better and faster aid response systems. We often see ordinary people step up heroically and help others during and after natural disasters.

The next time you find yourself facing a crises or difficult situation, remember the following opportunities:

- Remember that you can cope with anything that comes your way.
- See things in a new perspective and embrace what you have.
- Support where you can and shine as a light in the darkest of times.
- With every crisis comes opportunities!
- Push through the fear and be a hero!

Why Do Bad Things Happen?

From a science and engineering background, I like to think of problems as having a cause and a solution. After all the reading, research, and life I have experienced so far, the universe doesn't always work that way, and I have come to grips with the fact that some things—like why bad things happen—are beyond my understanding. I am uncomfortable expressing or imposing any of my religious beliefs. I also am not qualified to opine on Karma or other metaphysical beliefs about causality. There are some truths about why bad things happen, which include causes from bad decisions, natural disasters, random events, and immoral, amoral, or malicious intent.

We can all agree that some bad decisions can have if not direct causes for bad things then at least contributing factors. After smoking two packs of cigarettes per day for forty years, if you develop lung cancer you might consider the decision to start smoking a bad decision regarding your health. If you drink a twelve pack of beer or a bottle of whiskey per day for years and develop a liver problem, you might consider the decision to drink alcohol a bad decision. When you decide that you do not want to work for someone else and do not want to start your own business and find yourself financially strapped, you might not have made the best financial decisions. After spending years being abusive to your spouse and/or kids, you find yourself living alone and feeling lonely, especially around the holidays. Maybe you could have decided to be a better spouse or parent. In some cases, when you ask yourself, "Why did this happen to me?" be honest with yourself, and you might have the answer if you have made some bad decisions.

If you never decide that you want to do better, improve your situation, and take steps to achieve your dreams and goals, don't be surprised if you are in the same situation years down the road. Don't be too hard on yourself though. We all make bad decisions at times and eventually deal with the consequences. Think of how awesome it is that we can make new, better decisions, and have control over the immediate quality of our lives and the portions of our future that are still within our control!

Make sure you don't blame yourself for bad things that happen with no reasonably possible cause from you. Sometimes bad things come about from natural disasters, such as hurricanes, floods, tornados, blizzards, earthquakes, and droughts. You can try to be prepared for the first one you face or extra prepared for the next ones. Sometimes they come with little or no warning at all. You can still learn from each event and get better prepared for the next one but never escape the potential for bad things to happen from natural disasters. Does it help to find blame for the weather?

Many bad things can be attributed to random acts. We try to understand why things happen so we can have a target for our anger, assign blame, or otherwise make sense of why. The otherwise healthy person who suddenly dies from a heart attack. Someone with no high-risk behavior or habits that is diagnosed with cancer. The animal that runs into the street that causes a car crash that kills a young mother. The six-month-old infant who develops a brain cancer. These are the types of bad things that leave us struggling at times to find a reason. My only suggestion is that sometimes there is no why. In those cases, to where do we direct our anger? Maybe just at the situation itself?

People who are immoral, amoral, or have malicious intent can also cause bad things. Many would define this as or attribute it to just plain evil. My concern with the label of just evil is that it doesn't really leave any room for making things better and preventing more of the same. Is the act of a youth randomly killing someone as a gang initiation evil, or are there mitigating factors as to why the youth might feel desolate and needs a gang? Maybe that youth has a mental condition, was orphaned, or abused. When the dictator of a country commits genocide in support of self-improvement, power, and wealth, is that just evil? Are there contributing factors that we can look for and address next time that can be mitigated to reduce the chance of these acts happening again? I don't think that Adolf Hitler considered himself evil. I also don't think that Ted Bundy or Jeffrey Dahmer considered themselves evil. Does just plain evil leave any room for either preemptive attempts at changing someone's views, behavior or future acts, or room for redemption or forgiveness? I am not suggesting that any of the aforementioned people deserve any forgiveness or chance at redemption, but maybe the adult or teenager who made one bad decision or mistake might warrant forgiveness and a chance at doing better.

I know we do not always know why all bad things happen, and I suppose never will. Sometimes we do, other times we have an idea why, and the rest is a mystery. A healthy attempt to understand why so that we can avoid or mitigate bad things from happening is helpful. Other than ascribing blame for a target of anger, punishment, or justice, does it really help? Will the anger, punishment, or justice really help? I suppose a better man than I might always say no.

As much as you might think that understanding why a bad thing happened will help, you might challenge yourself by asking if that will really help. Where is your energy best spent? If you lost someone, how do you best honor them? Grieving for a time is natural. Temporary anger from the pain of a loss or injury is understandable. You have a responsibility to yourself, your family, and close ones to be the best you can be on their behalf. Ask yourself, "What would a hero do?"

Chapter Summary

- You are not alone; others have faced similar crises.
- There are tools for you to help you cope better.
- From crisis comes opportunity.
- You cannot always understand why bad things happen.
- Spend your time and energy doing the best you can.

Doing More; Doing Better

- A rising tide lifts all boats.
- Life is not a zero-sum game; when you give, you gain.
- "A noble spirit embiggens us all."—Lisa Simpson
- Can't you be the hero, at least sometimes?
- You can do and be as much better as you want to!

Now that you hopefully have some motivation to dream, set goals, and manage crises better, how are you going to help people and in turn help yourself?

When you get to be a big star, a billionaire, or what you consider the "top of the world," will you give back some to charities or otherwise help people? Why just then, why not now? Is it because then you will have extra to give? What about the things that you have in abundance now?

You don't have to be Mother Theresa to make a difference. You don't have to be a billionaire to give some back and try to make the world a better place. In fact, you don't have to sacrifice or have helping others cost you anything at all. You can be of benefit to others and actually gain yourself instead of lose anything.

What does it cost for you to tell someone they did a good job on something? How does it hurt you to humbly ask for help with something instead of arrogantly demand assistance? Does it really cost you anything to be polite?

Some people believe in Karma, or as I understand it, what you give out to the universe it sends back to you, good with good, bad with bad.

Other people have religious belief that dictates being good to others. Some are just naturally pleasant and want to help others. Then there are the self-serving, narcissistic MFs (me-firsts) and/or angry, rude-all-the-time people. Which of the types would you rather be friends with, work for, hire, or spend time with? With whom would you be more likely to do business? If you are a waiter or waitress at a restaurant, customer service representative at a car dealership, a doctor, nurse, or bank loan officer, which type of person are you likely to give faster and better service?

I understand sometimes feeling angry with situations or people. Short term, I think expressing anger can help you move things forward in certain situations. Personally, I am not angry often and do not feel comfortable expressing anger. To me, the opposite of happiness is not sadness; it is anger. From what I have read, heard, and believe, anger comes from fear and pain. In some cases, it becomes a habitual response for some people whenever they hear something they don't like or have just become so sour from past hurts that they know no other way to be.

During a radio interview in Maine about our support groups, I mentioned a term I had developed for some doctors who I have found prevalent also in many professions and walks of life: TWEPS. While it has its technical definition based on men, it can also be found to describe some women. It is an attempt to describe why some people feel that they have to belittle you in order to feel superior. My theory is the cause for this type of behavior and other bullying behavior is person with a low self-esteem.

When they asked me what TWEPS stood for, I told them that they probably didn't want me to say over the radio. They pressed me so I told them: teeny weeny eeny peeny syndrome. They asked!

For us, with hopefully better self-esteems, we should be able to help people with what we say. Give encouragement when we see it is needed. Tell someone you think they have a talent for something. Acknowledge people when they help you. Think about what you say before you say it. You can do a lot of good with words and positive comments. It doesn't cost you anything. It can pay dividends in the future. Good teachers recognize this and often have students come back years later to thank them. Part of the reason I have been able to write this book is because my dad has told me he thinks I have a talent for writing. One of my college professors who taught technical writing also told me that that I write good (ha!). Sometimes it is the little things that we can use to fire the efforts to reach the big dreams.

Life is not a zero-sum game, even though Wikipedia states on the subject: "Many people have a cognitive bias toward seeing situations as zero-sum, known as zero-sum bias."[17] My understanding of "zero sum" is that it assumes for someone to gain, someone has to lose. People who think of life in these terms feel they have to take from someone else in order for them go achieve. They step on others, demean them when it fits them, are prone to stealing ideas and credit and live what I believe are low-value lives.

The opposite of a zero-sum game philosophy is the theory expressed by the saying "a rising tide lifts all boats." In this model, when you help someone else, you are helping yourself. Again, back to the earlier thought that the business of business is people and that we succeed by helping and/or pleasing people. Also, there are things that can be given that are unlimited, for example, love and encouragement. Other things that can be of high value to the recipient but not cost to give are knowledge and wisdom. The theory being, again, a rising tide lifts all boats—help one, help all.

How much better off would you be if you knew back when what you know now? What would the impact be on your sharing with someone younger your wisdom and some of your experiences? What if you could find a mentor who knows a lot of what you need to learn?

"No one is an island" is listed as an inspiration point at the beginning of the chapter Dealing Better with Crises. Everyone deals with other people at some point. Your successes, failures, actions, and words affect not only you but the people around you. I remember a story from one of the motivational tapes I listened to years ago. The following is a paraphrased fictional story I heard from an audio tape that I believe was from Zig Ziglar:

A man works hard all day at his job at a manufacturing plant, and at the end of the day his manager yells at him, saying, "You didn't meet quota today. If you don't start doing better, I'm gonna have to let you go." The man goes home, sees his eldest son playing the *Call of Duty* video game. The father yells at him, "You are never going to amount to anything hanging around playing those stupid games. Get a job and a life because you can't stay here forever." The oldest son goes up to his younger brother's room and shuts the laptop with which his brother was working on a school project and says, "That's stupid. Why are you wasting your time with that? Don't you have a girlfriend you could be talking to?" The younger brother storms out of his room, sees and kicks the family dog and says, "I bet you have been up to no good all day. Isn't there something better you could be doing?" Now, wouldn't it have been more efficient if the plant manager had just gone to his employee's house and kicked the dog? What might have happened differently if the manager had said, "Good job today! We will catch up on the quota tomorrow."

If You Could Do It Again, How Would You Do It Better?

If I could go back in time, there are two the things I would most like to correct. The first is the bullying I did in high school to protect my own fragile self-image left over from being bullied myself a few years earlier. The second would be to have stepped up and prevented others from being bullied, especially by a friend of mine.

I remember when we were in junior high school we shared the bus with the high school kids, one of which took it upon himself to try to terrorize me with name calling. It didn't really bother me much, but my just taking it is probably what did the most damage to my self-esteem at the time. Or maybe that is just how I can rationalize the bullying I did in high school. I have since met some of the people I bullied and apologized with profound regret. I also reached out twenty-plus years later to one person from high school who I heard years later had apparently done some bullying and/or physical tormenting in a professional position of authority. From what I heard, one or more of his bullying victims had caught up with him out of his protective work environment and beat him close to death.

When I finally reached out via the internet and found him living in the Midwest, I contacted him by email, confirmed who he was, and said that I was really sorry how I treated him in high school. His answer was, "I don't know what you mean." My answer to that was, "Of course you wouldn't; you always were a better man than I was." I feel much better after I reached out and have forgiven myself blaming on my youth and being bullied earlier myself. I am sure apologizing doesn't make up for it, but it is something.

I still remember though one of the kids on the bus being bullied by my friend. He had a look of terror on his face that I will never forget. He had been a friend of mine in early grammar school. He was an extremely gentle person with a good heart but had some emotional development issues. He did not deserve the verbal abuse and torment he received from my friend. Looking back, I suppose my friend had his own self-esteem issues that could explain his behavior to some degree. I wish more than anything that I had stood up to my friend and told him to back off with the tormenting. Mark S., if by chance you ever read this, I am truly sorry and should have done better.

We need to remember as we live our lives and make our decisions that this life is not an audition or a trial run. Life is the real thing. Once we have done something (or failed to do something), that moment is gone. While you can't relive moments and you shouldn't concentrate on could have, should have, and would have, we do get to learn from our decisions and do better in the future.

Some of you reading this may have your own self-critical things in the past or recent bad behavior or decisions. The good news is you can use these things to inspire and motivate yourself to do better. If faced with some things that you failed with in the past, how would you do better? Are there things you wish you could atone for by doing better? It has been said that the hardest lessons are those best learned.

I recently found a list online of twenty-five hard lessons people learn from life from Power of Positivity.com (see the following). While I do not necessarily completely agree with every one, there is a lot of truth in them, and they help me make a point. How many hard lessons can you think of that may have prompted someone to list these? How many hard lessons have you learned that have you agreeing with some of these? Each statement below is from the website,[18] but the comments following each are from me:

1. "Not everyone is your friend." Unfortunately, people have their own agendas. Be careful who you trust! Also remember that no one is an island, and the risk of trusting is often worth it.

2. "If you don't stand for something you will fall for anything." If you don't have any values or convictions, what will guide your decisions? Stick to and defend your values! When all is said and done, make sure your decisions and actions make you proud!

3. "Doing wrong is always easier than doing right." I don't think that this is always the case. It is always true that doing the wrong thing is always wrong and doing the right thing is always right!

4. "Choose your friends wisely." Sometimes the people closest to you can be your biggest disappointments. If you want good friends, choose wisely and be a good friend yourself.

5. "Love doesn't always last forever." Not all love is true love. You may not know the difference at the time, and this can be a hard lesson to learn. Keep in mind though that some love, true love, is possible and can last forever!

6. "Some folks are worth fighting for." Not only are some people worth fighting for but some ideals and values are worth fighting for as well. You get to make the choice of who and what to fight for! Be a champion! Be a hero!

7. "Those closest to you can hurt you the most." No matter how much you trust someone close to you, keep in mind that they can hurt you the most. Keep in mind though that life is about risks, and the best things in life can have risks that hurt the most.

8. "You need to balance work and play." I wholeheartedly agree and would add to remember to have all aspects of life in balance. While the song from a single instrument may be enjoyable, think of the wonderous combination of multiple instruments

in the form of a band or an orchestra! It is not just the intensity of one aspect of life that counts. Each of the different aspects complement each other and help make life whole!

9. "Never jump to conclusions or make assumptions." While this may be true (unless you have that invention from the guy in *Office Space*), feel free to let your previous experiences and intuition guide you in your decisions.

10. "High school and college aren't the best times of your life." I suppose that might not be the case for a select few people, but in any event, the best times of your life are up to you! You have so much more wonderous exciting experience and life ahead of you! Don't look back!

11. "It's okay to ask a lot of questions." While I agree, keep in mind that you need to use tact in asking questions and try not to be perceived as grilling someone. You might consider prefacing your questions with something like: so I can better understand your/our situation, is it okay if I ask you some questions? When I was in sales I had some success with adding: Is it okay if I asking you multiple questions so I can best understand some of the whys behind your whats?

12. "Always read the fine print." They say the devil is in the details. You can have the best trust and understanding with someone and agree, but unless what you agree to is in writing, how can you be sure you both agree to the same thing? Someone may tell you one thing but in the written agreement it states something else. Trust no one implicitly. As Ronald Reagan said about the Soviet Union with the paraphrase of a Russian proverb: "Trust but verify."

13. "Never date those you work with." I am not sure about this one because I have never done it. Probably a general good rule to follow, but then again, you might miss out on a soul mate. Be cautious and don't risk more than you are willing to lose!

14. "Your happiness is not dependent on the opinions of others." This is definitely true in the short run. Your long-term happiness and success depend on your ability to please or otherwise help

others with goods and/or services. Never forget those you meet and how you treated them on your way up because you are likely to see them again if you slip back down for a while.

15. "Never do business with family or friends." Again, I am not fond of absolutes such as "never." Do be careful though; you have more to lose if things go wrong. I do know of some very successful businesses that continue with friend and family partners. At least you have a better basis for some trust.

16. "College isn't always a requirement." This is correct. There have been many very successful people with little or no formal education. The ability to learn and how to communicate with others are very important, and formal education can help with both.

17. "You don't have to like everyone." You may meet some people who for some reason or another you don't like. While you may not like them, you may still need to deal with them and/or respect them. For me, those I like least are the ones that express the arrogance and self-centeredness that I had myself in my youth. If you find yourself not liking someone, you might ask yourself why.

18. "It's easy to fall in love but hard to get over." I expect that is mostly because to fall in love and have your heart be filled feels much better than to have your heart feel broken when a relationship ends. Keep in mind, the pain of a break-up may never completely go away, but it will get better with time.

19. "People are struggling worse than you." Most definitely. See the "Estes theory of relativity" in the chapter "The Key to Your Success Is Your Attitude": no matter how bad you have it, someone has it worse. In the extreme, check the obituaries. You have it better than the people you find listed there. Think of your existing struggles. Are they really that bad? Sometimes they are, but keep in mind you are here to be able to deal with them.

20. "Your parents weren't wrong about most things." I think that most lasting things that you learn from your parents such as

values, character, how to be polite, your ABCs, and how to treat others are all good and they were right. Eventually, you grow to understand that what they were telling you was not only right but also in your best interest to know it.

21. "You don't know everything." I learned this at about age twenty-five and am much better for it. Once you realize this you will be more effective. You will ask for help, do the research you need, and have a lot more success. The most successful business CEOs and presidents surround themselves with people who know more and are better at things than they are.

22. "Rock bottom is meant to teach you a lesson." There is also a bright side to hitting rock bottom: the only way to go from there is up! I am not trivializing catastrophic rock-bottom failure, but from there you will learn valuable lessons and can use it to propel you farther and faster to something better than you otherwise would have gone.

23. "True friends are hard to come by." Value your true friends by being the best friend to them that you can be, and hopefully they will treat you the same. Be there for your friends, and they will be there for you.

24. "Your first love probably won't be your last." I am glad they included "probably," and this is true. You may not see it at the time since we all know that "love is blind," but keep in mind if you lose that first love, there are more chances out there for you to find love, maybe the one true love you deserve!

25. "Nothing is for certain in life." I agree that this is mostly true except for the cliché of death and taxes. There is also the fact that change is certain to occur at some point, and nothing stays the same forever. You can't be completely sure about anything, but make sure that you can handle the worst-case setback or disappointment.

If you could do it all again and already had learned the hard lessons above, how much better could you do? Well, you have the wonderful opportunity of hindsight to help guide you going forward with the knowledge and wisdom you gained for your next time. You can also share your wisdom and experiences with youths and others facing similar situations, trials, and challenges. Even if that other person has nothing direct to give you in return, you can find value in helping them. Not only are you able to make some additional good come from your experience, but you can feel better about yourself for making the most of it.

Do Better, but Don't Expect Perfection

Striving to do better for excellence in behavior, attitude, work, and life is a habit. It is also a way of life. Again, the great news is that is within your control. The only real failure is not to try. If you continue to try to do better, you will do so. With any luck, the setbacks you have will be minor and/or at least be valuable learning experiences. So many people have learned hard lessons in the past that there is a tremendous amount of wisdom to be gained from their trials. You will not be perfect. If you were perfect, you would not learn the hard lessons that will drive your successes. It also not reasonable to expect perfection.

A long time ago in the Persian Empire, Persian tribe members would work for years to make a single rug depicting their tribe's trials and tribulations. Their work was beautiful. From what I understand, they were deeply religious. In each of these rugs, they would intentionally include a flaw to signify that man is imperfect, signifying that only God can be perfect. Another way to think about the Persian flaw is: "To strive for perfection is noble; to expect perfection is blasphemy." Give yourself a break when you have a flaw. Overcome your flaws and strengthen other areas to compensate, if you can. Again, you are not perfect, but you can do and get better. One of the best ways to improve is to learn from others' experiences and hopefully gain wisdom that others suffered greatly to obtain.

Often we tend to remember bad things we have done or bad things others have done without remembering the good. We also often focus on the negative, maybe because our instinct is to correct or make up for negative situations. Sometimes to avoid things getting worse we have to take immediate drastic actions focusing on negative behavior or situations. Focus your efforts on things within your control and let go of the things that are not. There is an old prayer called the Serenity Prayer, which addresses this topic well: "Lord, give me the serenity to accept the things I cannot change, courage to change the things I can, and the wisdom to know the difference."

Sometimes we seem to remember our mistakes and our setbacks more than our successes. In the right context of learning from our mistakes, that can help us. Other times, when we are considering taking a risk on a new venture or approaching a person with a request, if we remember only the previous difficulties or failures, we can let it shake our confidence. What if you can forgive yourself for not being perfect and also gain confidence from knowing what you learned from your last setback? Use the fact that you know that you are imperfect to continuously get better each time you learn more.

We all tend to worry about things that might happen. For some things, we can affect the likelihood of them happening; others we cannot. The more energy we waste concentrating on things outside our control, the less we have to manage the things within our control. Worry and fear can be crippling, yet it is prudent to plan for events that reasonably might happen. I suggest that the best way to proceed is to be prepared for the worst-case outcome but hope and act toward making the best case. Even if you wanted to, can you really foresee all of the potential things that could happen, including obstacles or problems? It is good common sense to consider likely possibilities and be prepared for them within reason, but don't waste mental energy or other resources on things that may never happen. Nothing seems to ever happen perfectly, and allow for the fact that you will have to adjust as you go along.

Take Responsibility and Authority

We are all responsible for our choices and actions. Our choices and actions dictate our long-term circumstances. We all tend to want to come up with excuses at times for why we cannot or could not do something. In order to protect our own fragile self-esteem, it is easier to blame other people and things outside our control.

Hellen Keller (1880–1968) lost her sight and hearing at nineteen months old. She eventually became an author of fourteen books and other writings and a social activist. She also traveled to over thirty different countries. If ever anyone had good excuses to not try, it was Helen Keller, yet she decided early on to take responsibility for having a meaningful, productive life instead of wallowing in self-pity for circumstances beyond her control. Can you imagine the strength of character it took for her to work to better herself and contribute to society? I have news for you. You have the same strength and sense of purpose. You just need to find the right ways to tap into them and imagine what you can accomplish!

If we take responsibility for our actions and situations, we can celebrate our successes, fix our own problems, and navigate our own destinies. When we blame and cede our responsibility to others, we not only lose control but lose any authority over our lives. Just as responsibility and authority go hand in hand in business, so, too, do they in life in general.

The guaranteed way not to succeed is to not act at all.

> "Inaction breeds doubt and fear. Action breeds confidence and courage. If you want to conquer fear, do not sit home and think about it. Go out and get busy."
> —Dale Carnegie

The only true failure is not to try. We all have our reasons why we don't act: fear, excuses, obstacles, haven't decide which actions to pursue. Not only can these reasons be crippling, but they have the second-order effect of helping you to feel discouraged because you haven't done anything yet. Do something, anything at all, and you can have the opposite effect. Once you do some things and take some steps, you are not only on your way and have actually done something but you will feel better and empowered to do more. Even setbacks and identifying challenges to your goals are accomplishments in and of themselves. Spend a half hour researching online how to do things you want to do. There is a tremendous amount of free information out there. You can find that someone has done something similar, how they did it, and maybe figure out how to do better.

In preparation for writing this book, I decided to read at least ten new books about doing better and being better. Since then, I have read twenty and have another four in a stack near my bed ready to read. I have developed a habit of reading about a half hour per night at bedtime. Most of the books I bought used online for five to seven dollars, including delivery. Others my wife has bought for me at antique or thrift stores for similar prices. You can check these types books out at your local library. It doesn't take a whole lot of time or money to do a little learning or research each day, and it can help you feel better about your progress toward your goals. How many times do you need to try in order to succeed? Keep trying, stick to it, and you will do it.

Thomas Edison patented the first practical incandescent light bulb in 1879, which was the standard light bulb for over a hundred years. It took him over ten thousand tries before he got it right. Granted, from what I understand, he had assistants helping with a lot of the tries, but still, ten thousand? At what point do you give up? How can you think you can do better than the first five thousand tries? Apparently, he was ridiculed, and when asked by a reporter, "How did it feel to fail ten thousand times?" Edison replied, "I didn't fail ten thousand times. The light bulb was an invention with ten thousand steps."

Another example of persistence that I want to include in this book also shows that it is never too late in life to have big dreams and work hard. Harland Sanders (a.k.a. Colonel Sanders). At age sixty-five, he had developed what he thought was a special recipe for fried chicken (Kentucky Fried Chicken, or KFC). After failing at his own restaurant, he tried to sell his recipe to other restaurants. I have read that he failed over one thousand times until he found one that would work with him. Today there are over twenty thousand KFC restaurants in the world spread out over 119 countries. Not only did Harland persevere through the one-thousand-plus rejections but he started the whole venture at the age most people have already retired!

How many times are you willing to try? With each attempt you learn more and can do better the next time. Who or what was it that drove the persistence of Edison and Col. Sanders? I expect that they did not have life coaches keeping them motivated. I don't think that they had anyone else they had to answer to for motivation to keep going. Did they have an innate drive? Were they obsessed with success? Were they always that way or did they take it upon themselves to take action then learn some ways to do better and be better?

They took it upon themselves as their responsibility as per their authority to do so. No one but you is going to push you to do greatness the way you need to be pushed. Let your desire drive your inspiration, motivation, action, learning, perseverance, progress, and success!

Remember: you don't have to. You get to!

Chapter Summary

- Do better, but don't expect perfection.
- If you could go back in time, what would you do better?
- How can you use what you have learned to help someone else do better?
- You have the ultimate responsibility and authority for your behavior and goals.
- Become a persistent force of nature, and nothing will stop you!

Do Better with Balance

- "Disharmony at home or work is toxic to a person's physical disposition and mental health."— Kilroy J. Oldster.
- "Success in life is useless if you don't have a balance of happiness, peace, hope, and optimism."— Germany Kent.
- What is financial success without the health to enjoy it?
- Enjoy the ride, not just the destination!
- You spend most of your time along the way—relish it!

So, you want to be better. Are you ready to do better in order to make that happen? You can be on track and doing the work toward your primary goals, but what about the other aspects of your life? Are you keeping things in balance? How much longer can you continue toward your goals if you don't maintain your health? If you don't provide for yourself and your family the basic needs, how long will you continue? What about your other roles as spouse, parent, child, employee, friend?

Make sure you don't succeed in one area of life to the detriment of other areas. We have all seen movies or know people who have out-of-balance lives and eventually something blows up or at best they maintain success in one area but are miserable. A man works all hours of the day and weekends to try to do better, and his lonely wife finds comfort in the arms of another man. Both parents work long hours, travel, and wonder why their kids rebel and fail at school.

It is not just the goal or end game. It is as much or not more about the process and the journey along the way. Life isn't just about accomplishments; it is about your personal growth, your quality of

Life, and your impact on other people. You need to maintain some balance in your life. You don't find too many one or two-legged chairs or tables.

If all you do is work hard at something hour by hour, day by day, week by week, and so on, with no time to relax, take care of your health, or spend time with family and/or friends, you may have success, but how is your overall life? Even worse, if you don't take care of your health, how can you expect to be at your best to work on your other goals? No matter how much you might enjoy your primary work focus, I propose that you will miss out on a large portion of what life has to offer you if you don't take not much time for other aspects of life too.

If you have a car with a tire that is out of balance, you may not notice all the time. At certain speeds, though, there can be anywhere from a minor vibration to a violent shake that can cause damage. In my mechanical engineering courses, I learned about harmonics and natural frequencies. This is the phenomenon in which certain systems have natural frequencies—revolutions per minute, occurrences per time, cycles—at which when things are out of sync there can be a major disruption. With cars, it often seems you feel tire imbalance between 20 and 30 mph and between 60 and 70 mph.

Life has its own cycles, rhythms, and balances. Health, family, learning, career, goals, recreation, mental health, spiritual health, financial health, and others are all important to us in different ways. When something is out of balance, the system doesn't work well. Sometimes you hear of someone having a midlife crisis. It could be a man or woman who is now an empty-nester after the kids are gone or someone whose spouse has left them because they spend no time at home. In any event, it is difficult to go along smoothly, climb, and do better when something is out of balance in your life either way too much, not enough, or nonexistent.

You have issues with a family member and are estranged, then a crisis or death in the family comes up, and now you have a tough time connecting. You have a great opportunity to take a trip you have always want to do, but you have neglected your health and aren't healthy enough to go. A great business opportunity comes along, but you haven't been saving any money or paying bills on time so your finances and poor credit restrict you. All it takes is one self-imposed crisis to knock your life out of balance, and it always seem to come at the worst time or "natural frequency," when other things are happening too. Does it sometimes feel that a lot of bad things seem to happen at the same time? If your life is built on only one strong aspect like a successful career, what happens when you have a health issue, a family crisis, or other area of your life you have been neglecting has a challenge?

Along with keeping balance in our lives, we need to keep in mind that the majority of our lives is spent in the pursuit of our dreams or goals not just at our destination. Much of our life involves struggles, trials, and challenges. Instead of feeling like something is knocking you out of balance because you don't have other strong areas of your life, how much better can you be if you have family, friends, or other resources to help support you?

If we are not growing, we are dying. The only way to coast is downhill. So, as we continue to strive to do better and accomplish more, we need to make sure we are enjoying our efforts. It is the failures that help us appreciate the successes. It is our efforts that we are proud of that make us feel valuable. We don't need to enjoy the hourly daily grind of the hard work, but we can feel like we are being productive, making the right choices, and doing better.

"We enjoy the process far more than the proceeds." Warren Buffet, multibillionaire and cofounder of the Giving Pledge, inspires other successful people to give to philanthropic causes.

We can spend so much of our time working toward goals that we think will make us happy that sometimes we miss out on being happy while we are working. Either because we do not have balance in our lives or we do not have the right goals. It seems to some of us that not much has happened, and all of a sudden ten or twenty years or more have gone by, and it feels like nothing important or much enjoyment has occurred.

As I am writing this section of the book, I just returned from a funeral service for a father of a childhood friend from the neighborhood where

I grew up. I am again feeling reminded of my own mortality and some truths and wisdom I have considered in the past. We each want to maximize the overall value of our lives. In considering this with brain tumor and cancer patients in the past with my engineering, science, and math background, I put this into a math formula. I formulated years ago that the overall value of our lives is the quantity of our lives multiplied by the quality of our lives:

$$\text{Life Value} = \text{Life Quantity} \times \text{Life Quality}$$

It seems more urgent to try to maintain the quality of life when we are facing impending limits on the quantity (diagnosed with cancer, facing bypass surgery following a heart attack, etc.), especially when the quantity looks to end. The sad part is that we have so much more time to work on our quality of life when we seem to have plenty of quantity but we don't. Ironically, if you don't have balance in your life with maintaining your health, you reduce the quality of your life but also the quantity.

Along with becoming better as you work toward your goals and increase the quality of your life as you do so, how else are you to increase your quality and value? Earlier in this book I talked about how people are compensated when they please or help other people. In that case, I was talking about business models and how you make money by providing goods and services to others. Your compensation in that model is money. You want the money so that you can enrich your life, improve the quality, and have the resources to work on maintaining and extending your life.

How about we consider that you can modify the business model so you improve the quality of your life at times but don't need to be paid money in order to do so. What are some of the things you value? Do you enjoy the status of being appreciated? How about knowing that you made a major positive difference in someone's life? What is your worth if you can improve the quality of one person per day, ten people per day, or more? What would that do to the quality of your life?

I suggest there is a better model than work hard in business, make lots of money, then, if you feel like it, give some money back to society in the form of helping people by donating to charities and worthwhile causes. You don't have to spend money or even any significant time to be of value to others long and short term. You certainly don't have to be financially wealthy or rich. You also do not have to compromise your efforts toward your primary goals. If anything, I think you will find by helping others, even in small ways, will help you. How much more productive will you be when you have a better attitude about yourself? How much better will you sleep knowing you did some direct good earlier in the day?

One thing that you can do is if you see someone has a talent, point it out to them, and mention that you admire it. Maybe ask them whether they have ever thought about using their talent to do more professionally or to help others more. You never know who you might inspire for greatness. You help yourself when you help others, and it doesn't have to cost you.

Chapter Summary

- Stay in balance.
- Enjoy the ride of life!
- Life Value = Life Quantity × Life Quality.
- You don't have to wait to do good things and make a difference!
- Help others; help yourself.

Have a Better Quality of Life

- Don't you deserve the best?
- You are capable of much better!
- Don't your loved ones deserve the best you?
- You can do and be much better!
- Decide to have a better quality of life and you will!

I heard a song with great lyrics a couple of years ago, and I have thought about it many times. It has a lot of well-wishing statements. The tile of the song is "Have It All" by Jason Mraz. The message is great, and the music in the song is very upbeat. The question that comes up for me while listening to this song is, What are my best times now, and how can I make them better for the future?

You may have heard the phrase coined by Margaret Wolf Hungerford in the late 1800s: "Beauty is in the eye of the beholder." Each person has their own view of what is beautiful to them. What some see as beauty others may see as chaos, ugliness, plainness, or other non-beauty. From a recent search online, I found that there has been significant debate over whether quality is in the eye of the beholder. I see merit in the arguments for and against but propose a more useful way to look at quality: quality is in the eye of the result and impacts the reviewer. Unlike beauty, quality can be defined and must be defined in order to have any meaningful assessment and improvement of quality.

How do you know if you are doing better or if something is of higher quality? What is better quality? Which is a higher quality car, one that lasts for three hundred thousand miles plus or one that gets over forty miles to the gallon or one with a quiet, smooth ride? How do you improve the quality of your product, your relationships, your marriage, your life?

There is a term used in business: total quality management or "TQM." According to a source I found online during searches about quality (Pharmatutor – Pharmacy Infopedia)[19]:

TQM is a business management system, which:

- Focuses on meeting owners'/customers' needs by providing quality services at a cost that provides value to the owners/customers
- Is driven by the quest for continuous improvement in all operations
- Recognizes that everyone in the organization has owners/customers who are internal or external
- Views and organization as a system with a common aim rather than as individual departments acting to maximize their own performances
- Focuses on the way tasks are accomplished rather than simply what tasks are accomplished
- Emphasizes teamwork and a high level of participation by all employees.

There are books, seminars, courses, business division departments, speakers, and careers devoted to TQM for businesses, including manufacturing, health care, and other industries. Why might you care? Because there is a lot of wisdom from TQM that you can use to help you maximize your quality of life. Many tactics, systems philosophies, and wisdom used to improve the quality of businesses can be used or adapted to help you improve the quality of your life.

Early in my career I learned about TQM by being introduced to and reading *The Deming Management Method* by Mary Walton. It is about a system for improving quality by the engineer and consultant W. Edwards Deming. Deming's method was developed to improve the quality of manufacturing and business, which included the fourteen points listed below. I have added notes after each to do my best to paraphrase how you might adopt each point to improve your quality of life.

Deming's fourteen points[20] underlined in quotes, my adds after:

1. <u>"Create a constancy of purpose for improving produces and services."</u> Define and document your values, what is important to you, and what you want to be better. List what you want and what you want to better.

2. <u>"Adopt the new philosophy."</u> Commit to improving quality and doing better in all things even when no one is looking. If you walk by a piece of trash, pick it up. If you need help, ask for it. If you want to learn, research it. If you want to do better at something, learn how to and do it.

3. <u>"Cease dependence on inspection to improve quality."</u> Do not let others values or opinions of you define what is important to you and what quality means to you. You can ask for advice and review from others, but in the end, it is your assessment of what is better that should guide you.

4. <u>"End the practice of awarding business on price alone; instead, minimize total cost by working with a single supplier."</u> Try to build teams to help you do better and keep their interests in mind as you go, and you will improve your quality and their quality.

5. <u>"Improve constantly and forever every process for planning, production and services."</u> Do better wherever you can always in every aspect of your life that meets your core values and goals. Is it that much more effort to be a better husband while you are being a better parent? Are you not able to have a better attitude yourself while you are helping others with their attitudes?

6. <u>"Institute training on the job."</u> Learn as you go. Do better the next time based on what you have learned. Like Scotty from the original *Star Trek* said: "There is an old saying on Earth: Fool me once shame on you. Fool me twice shame on me."

Then Mr. Checkov says in his Russian accent: "I know this saying. It was invented in Russia." We do much better when we learn from our and others' experiences.

7. "Adopt and institute leadership." Lead your team(s) to do better: your family, your coworkers, people you meet. Set the tone with your attitudes. Show how doing better is in everyone's best interest. It does not lessen you to acknowledge and praise the success of others. A true leader surrounds themselves with people who are better and does not have to feel they are the best at everything.

8. "Drive out fear." Use whatever tools you can to eliminate action-suppressing, success-limiting fear. This includes getting rid of your fear of change, fear of failure, and fear of success. When you still have fear, move through it. Courage is not having no fear. It is moving forward regardless of fear.

9. "Break down barriers between staff areas." Try not to isolate other portions of your life while you improve one aspect. Don't think of being more healthy as an impediment to being a better husband or wife. Think of ways to have your spouse join you with walks, playing tennis, or going to the gym. Package your goals as win-win versus win-lose or zero-sum game. You don't need to sacrifice one area of your lift to do better in another.

10. "Eliminate slogans, exhortations and targets for the workforce." Here, I believe the statement is referring to banners such as "Zero Defects Today" and "Quality Counts." You should use positive signs and thoughts constantly confirming where you want to go and that you will get there. List specific features of your goals and your whys to help you stay inspired and motivated.

11. "Eliminate numerical quotas for the workforce and numerical goals for management." Having rigid numerical quotas by which you measure success does not serve the long-term success. Interim target goals are meant to be a guide by which you can gauge your progress toward your overall goals and feel some accomplishment of partial success.

12. "Remove barriers that rob people of pride and workmanship, and eliminate the annual rating of merit system." Stay away from the naysayer nonsupportive people in your life who drag you down, or at least let them know you would prefer support or even silence instead of negativity. Stamp out the negative thoughts that drag you down. You don't fail by not succeeding because of setbacks; you learn so you can do better. Keep the faith! You can! You will!

13. "Institute a vigorous program of education and self-improvement for everyone." Commit doing better. When you have a challenge, do what the Marines do: improvise, adapt, and overcome. Let each setback and each move forward be a learning experience to help you do better and be better!

14. "Put everyone in the company to work accomplishing the transformation." Take pride in your efforts to do better. Share your goals and efforts with those around you who are supportive. Help others feel good about themselves by being supportive of them, and in turn they will be more supportive to you.

I cannot help myself but to suggest that we can do even better by adding another point:

15. Share your successful quality improvement strategies with others, and try to inspire them to improve their own quality and to better. Be careful not to sound superior or tell them what you think they should do. Rather, suggest that they might do better based on some recent success that you have had or have heard that someone else has had.

As I was doing some research on quality and quality of life, I was listening to a radio station online and hearing the song from Nickelback called "Rockstar." In the song the singer mentions a list of things that are quality-of-life items that he wants. We may not all want to have a bathroom we can play baseball in or be rock stars, but we each have our own concept of what quality of life is and what better is. Some items are long term, such as making a bigger difference in the world, while some items are shorter term, such as being healthier. Some can be both immediate and long term such as being happy. Other quality-of-life issues may be less esoteric like being able to walk without pain or being able to get a good night's sleep. Medical professionals often try to take into account quality of life when deciding if life-sustaining medical care should be withheld for severely disabled or ill patients who are suffering.

The great news is that not only do you get to decide what quality of life means to you, but you are also the one in control of improving your quality of life! You can have family, friends, professionals, strangers, mentors, and others who can assist you with different levels of life-quality issues, but you are the team leader. You set the goals, decide what you want, what is best, and how you want it. Sometimes your options for maximizing your quantity of life are at odds with maximizing your quality of life. In the long term, if you smoke, abuse alcohol, and eat unhealthy foods, you may feel you have a higher quality of life, but those actions can shorten and reduce the quantity of your life. Other times, when you are dealing with quantity-of-life issues such as a cancer diagnosis for yourself or a loved one, you may have options for life-extending treatments that may drastically affect the quality of life. When you struggle with quality of life versus quantity of life, you may find it helpful to think again about the formula listed in an earlier chapter where I propose that the overall value of life depends on both the quality and the quantity of life. While we do have some control over the quantity of life, I think we have more control over our overall value of life by improving our quality of life.

How might you best maximize your quality of life? Consider making this a priority goal for yourself, and list the things that are important to you. Then list the things that you can do to improve the quality of those items and do better. Some examples might include that you want to:

1. feel less stressed
2. be less tired during the day
3. feel like your life has meaning
4. be in less physical pain
5. be in less emotional pain

6. enjoy life more
7. feel successful
8. be happier

By listing what is quality and what you want to improve, you are performing item #1 in that list and "creating a constancy of purpose." After you have your list of things that are quality-of-life issues, consider rereading each of the other fourteen items and make notes of how you might use each to improve your quality issues. I understand the natural tendency is to just take any suggestions like mine with a grain of salt and not bother to do anything, or at least not yet. If you truly want to improve the quality of life, I ask you: Why not try these tools and suggestions? What do you have to lose? If not now, then when? What do you expect to happen if you do nothing? What are you waiting for? Just do it! Do something! Do it now! Don't you deserve better?

Chapter Summary

- What is better quality of life to you?
- Improve your life with Total Quality (of life) Management tools.
- You have the awesome power to improve your quality of life!
- List the things you want to be better!
- Start now- what do you have to lose!

Do Better by Being More Optimistic

- Be optimistic about your future!
- Optimism is better that pessimism by definition!
- Without optimism how do you maintain hope?
- If you hope to do better, you can do better!
- "A pessimist sees the difficulty in every opportunity; an optimist sees the opportunity in every difficulty." —Winston Churchill

A big part of a better quality of life and doing better is being optimistic, which is something you can do if you choose to. A definition of optimism I found online is: "hopefulness and a confidence about of the future successful outcome of something" and "a philosophy that good things will happen."[21] Another way to look at optimism is that it is highlighting, focusing on, or concentrating on the positive. Pessimism, on the other hand, is highlighting, focusing on, or concentrating on the negative.

Again, back to Physics 101. In order for there to be an action or movement, there must be a force. For us to act, to do something, to work toward a goal, we need a force or something to motivate us to act. Inspiration to motivate us to act can come from our why, our sense of urgency, our desires, and hope that we can succeed. Optimism drives our hope that we can reach our goals and desires. It inspires us and motivates us to act.

Along with the fact that you see more positives and have more hope when you are optimistic, I found what I think is a good list online from "verywellmind"[22] of five reasons to be more optimistic (their list items are in quotes underlined, after are my comments):

1. "Optimists live longer: 11% to 15%." The more optimistic you are the less stress you typically have. With less stress comes lower incidents of heart attacks, strokes, and other illnesses. In extreme cases, if you are not optimistic or hopeful that your sickness or illness can be cured, you are less likely to go see doctors and others who may be able to help you. If you are not optimistic about the outcome of exercise, stopping a bad habit or avoiding unnecessary risks, the choices you make will likely shorten your life span.

2. "Optimists have better love lives." Who wants to be around a pessimist? Optimists are more fun to be around because they have more positive attitudes. Not only do optimists get better attitudes back from their significant others but they are more likely to attract more suiters when dating. Optimists focus on the positives in life and usually positives in others as well. Who wants to be around a pessimist pointing out your negatives and flaws?

3. "Optimists are more successful." Optimists see more opportunities that pessimists. The more opportunities you have the better the chances you will succeed. How do you put your heart into being successful with your dreams or goals without concentrating on the hopeful outcomes of your efforts? Optimists are more likely to learn from setbacks instead of being demoralized by seeing setbacks as failures.

4. "Optimists take fewer sick days." If you feel a little off when you wake up and start thinking it could be something serious that will get worse (like a pessimist would), you will likely call out sick than an optimist who might think a little off will get better during the day. An optimist looking forward to going to work and the best outcomes is much less likely to look for a reason to stay home than a pessimist.

5. <u>"Optimists bounce back faster."</u> You can't keep an optimist down. An optimist finds reasons to get back up and ways to do so. An optimist sees getting ground as an opportunity to be polished and shine. If you are not optimistic about continuing after a setback, how many setbacks will it take you before you give up?

From another list online by Life Optimizer[23] I have selected what I think are the best ten of the forty-five benefits of optimism they list:

1. It gives you a reason for living.
2. It promotes happiness.
3. It creates a sense of fulfillment and satisfaction.
4. It improves physiological and psychological well-being.
5. It gives you peace of mind.
6. It ensures that you believe in your dream.
7. It creates a positive attitude.
8. It increases your level of motivation.
9. It promotes self-confidence and boosts self-esteem.
10. It reduces the level of your frustration and worries.

Maybe you see or are starting to see the potential benefits of being more optimistic. How can you be more optimistic and reap the benefits of optimism? Here are the ABCs of being more optimistic as I see it:

A. Consider your situations in the right frame of mind or "paradigm" as discussed earlier in this book. Put a positive spin on things as you see them. You can find and highlight the positive in any situation with: "I am looking forward to when this is done," "This will be a great story to tell," or "At least it can't get any worse!"

B. Limit your time spent with pessimistic people. Spend more time with optimistic people. Do this with people in person and on social media. Both pessimism and optimism can be contagious.

C. Don't watch the news, or at least limit your time watching. It always seems to show and accentuate bad things that happen and negatives. I remember when trying to get some public service announcements out for our support group, mentioning to a TV reporter that the news seems to concentrate on murders and other negatives. She said that she enjoys reporting about murders because it is shocking.

D. Keep a journal or list of positive things. Maybe write down five or so each day. As I am writing this, I took a brief break to write in my planner:

   1. I am in good health.
   2. I have a family I can count on.
   3. I have the best and most supportive wife ever.
   4. I am making good progress with the book.
   5. I am getting some good help on another project.

E. You can acknowledge the negative and potential downsides and be prepared for them; just don't dwell on them. Practice optimism, not blind optimism.

F. Soften the blow. The next time someone cuts you off in traffic remember the last time you did the same thing, possibly by accident because you did not see them.

G. If you find that you compare yourself to others, remember how good you have it compared to many others:

   1. If you have a home, think of those who are homeless.
   2. If you have a family, think of those who don't.
   3. If you have your health, think others with cancer or worse.
   4. If you think you are having a bad day, read the obituaries.

H. Smile often (I am working on this myself). Smiles can be contagious and take the edge off. You tend to feel better and have a brighter outlook if you smile. Do you smile because you are happy, or are you happy because you smile?

I. Find the silver lining, the opportunity in the crises, the lesson in the hardship. A book I am reading now has a great way to look at this: poor people see difficulties in the opportunities, while rich people see opportunities in the difficulties.

J. Cut yourself some slack. If you don't do well, know that you can do better. No one is perfect, and we all make mistakes and have setbacks. What matters is how we deal with them.

K. Focus and put your energy into the solution instead of complaining about the problem. Decide that you can make things better, then figure out how to.

L. Don't be a victim. You have more power and control over your circumstances than you think. Know that you can do better. Take control of that which you can. Remember, your attitude is totally under your control.

M. Fake it until you make it. You may not feel very optimistic either based on a recent series of setbacks or a lot of negatives. In that case, decide that you will at least seem to be optimistic and highlight the positives anyway. You should still get some of the benefits of being sincerely optimistic; it will help you on your way to being optimistic.

N. Don't get trapped into a pity-party discussion comparing how bad you have it to others as they one up you to show how they have it worse. Maybe in that situation give them what they want and say, "Wow, that is much worse than I have it!" Maybe you will even feel better and a little more optimistic about your situation.

O. Keep in mind the "Law of Attraction": positive thoughts attract positive outcomes, while negative thoughts attract negative outcomes. Have you ever noticed that if your day starts badly with waking up late, or stormy weather, that your whole day seems to go bad, one thing after another? Consider that if you think you will have a bad day, you likely will.

P. Make a list of positive outcomes and successes you have had, and refer to it when you think you need a boost to your optimism. Sometimes we get caught up in the challenges and setbacks we face and forget how far we have come and how well we have done.

In the iconic movie comedy *Groundhog Day*, Bill Murry plays the role of Phil Connors, the main character, who starts out as a pessimistic, angry, unhappy, unsuccessful TV meteorologist sent to small Pennsylvania town to cover their Groundhog Day event. No matter what Phil does, he keeps waking up to repeat the same day over and over. He starts out getting more negative and pessimistic and even tries to kill himself multiple ways, but each morning waking up again to February 2, Groundhog Day. He tries half-heartedly to do better each day in the hope that if he gets the day right, he can move on to the next day, but to no avail. After giving up trying to do better to move on to the next day and just enjoying doing better and being better each day, lo and behold, he wakes up and it is the next day. At that point he is happy, has a relationship with his female colleague, the townspeople think he is great, and he seems to spread joy wherever he goes. Instead of loathing the town, the people in it, and everything about it, he decides he wants to stay there and be happy. Phil starts off in the movie as pessimistic, pointing out all the negatives of the small town, the people, and the weather. At the end of the movie, he is full of optimism, cheerful, and happy. My summary does not do the movie justice, but especially for a comedy, it has a great story and wisdom in it to help have more optimism and do better.

If you have any goals, dreams, or other aspirations, you must have at least some optimism that you can achieve them or that they can happen; otherwise, why try? I understand there are some potential downsides of being overly optimistic. If you don't consider any potential downsides, how can you be prepared for them if they occur? Who wants to be around the pessimistic one always pointing out the negatives like a Debby Downer from *Saturday Night Live*? Don't take the wind out of your own sails with pointing out negatives and being pessimistic or staying around others who are negative. Choose to find the positive, and you will find it.

You can to choose your outlook, what to hope for, what to work for, your attitude, and whether to smile. If you are pessimistic about your life, your week, or your day, what is your attitude like when you wake up in the morning? How do you approach your day, your work, or your family when you are pessimistic? I suggest that if you sincerely want to do better and be better that you hope for and find positives to fill your sails, put fire in your belly, and drive you forward, onward, and upward to your dreams and goals!

Chapter Summary

- Optimism drives your hope, inspiration, and motivation!
- You are happier when you are optimistic!
- There are many tools you can use to be and stay optimistic.
- Remember your past successes, and keep in mind you know more and are better now.
- Stay away from pessimistic people who bring you down.

Find Your Inspiration and Motivation to Do Better

- What is the spark of greatness in you?
- Find the spark, fan it, feed it, and let it drive your engine of success!
- You can have as much passion, drive, and heart as it takes to succeed; just find them and use them!
- You can be your biggest supporter!
- Use inspiration and motivation to fuel your journey!

As I write this portion of the book, I am struggling with my own inspiration and motivation issues. I am excited about the recent additional research on the subjects and some of the insights I have found that I will share with you. I think that the more we know about these forces the better we can find and use them. What are these forces that drive others to so much success? How can you and I find and tap into inspiration and motivation to fire our dreams, goals, aspirations, and success?

As I try to with most challenges or problems, I want to define what I am dealing with and research how to best proceed. I have struggled at times with the definitions of inspiration versus the definition of motivation. I found the latest definitions online from the freedicionary.com site,[24] which sites multiple sources:

Inspiration:[a]

1. The excitement of the mind or emotions to a high level of feeling or activity

2. A person or thing that moves the intellect or emotions or prompts action or intention
3. Stimulation of the mind, feelings, etc. to special or unusual activity or creativity
4. The state of being stimulated or aroused
5. A person or thing that inspires

Motivation:[b]

1. The act or process of motivating
2. The state of being motivated, having a desire or willingness to act
3. Desire to do; interest or drive
4. Incentive or inducement
5. The process that arouses, sustains and regulates human and animal behavior

I found a chart online from keydifferences.com[25] that seems to help me understand better the difference that includes the following:

BASIS	MOTIVATION	INSPIRATION
Force	Driving force	Pulling force
Sense of	Resistance	Excitement
Life	Short-lived	Everlasting
Feel	Compel	Propel
Source	External	Internal
Impulse	Deliberate	Spontaneous

I am not sure I agree with all of the chart, but it does provide some food for thought. In any event, what we need are methods and tools to make us to act, keep going, and do what we need to in order to accomplish our goals. It sounds simple enough, but will these tools and methods help drive us, especially when we need it most? What are these wonderful driving forces that help some of us succeed while others of us just continue to get by? If we better understand them, maybe we can better use them.

To me, inspiration is something that sparks a drive inside us that is a reason for us to want to do something. For example, my wife, Evelyn, inspires me to want to do better and do better because I love her and I feel that she deserves the very best of me and no less. When I remember this, it helps motivate me to act. Actions are what move us forward so we can get things done and accomplish our goals.

I am not sure exactly what kicked in and got me to actually start writing this book after years of thinking about it, drafting outlines, doing research on how to get published, and so on. I am pretty sure I just got fed up with my own lack of success and started re-visiting, researching, and developing new tools to move me forward. I had the inspiration for years and even felt motivated at times. I did some research, wrote a sample chapter, submitted it with an inquiry letter to an agent, and got some feedback, but it went nowhere for years. Eventually, I put a time goal on it and did that all-powerful act: I started actually writing and cranking out chapters. Now that I had a draft done, I had a publisher do a first edit and was ready to go to print. But I was unhappy with the draft, the total amount of content, and how effective it would be for people who wanted to do better. I needed motivation to continue, to make significant progress each day, and to be done within two months with an expanded draft.

Back to some of the things listed in previous chapters:

- What do you want?
- Why do you want it?
- Get control of your attitude.
- Make it real and set goals.
- Start doing better.
- Make steps for doing better.
- Act in accordance with the universal truths.
- Do better by choice.
- Do better with crises.
- Have a better quality of life.
- Understand the importance of optimism.

All of the above are great concepts and ideas that work, but what will actually get you to move forward, do better, be better, and reach your goals? Inspiration and motivation. These are the forces that drive us to act. Back to why people act and Maslow's hierarchy of needs; therein are the things that typically motivate us to act. From the basic necessities to our desires and goals, how do you get and stay inspired and motivated to start and keep going? I believe that inspiration is our *why* and our *we can* while motivation is our *what*, *how*, and *when*. I also believe that inspiration is the force that fires our motivation and that motivation is what drives us to do the all-powerful magic of action!

There is a song from the 1980s called "Magic Power" by the band Triumph that I still listen to often on YouTube while I am working. I find it somewhat inspiring. Other songs I find inspiring include the *Rocky* movies' theme songs, "Gonna Fly Now" and "Eye of the Tiger" and more contemporary songs such as Eminem's "Lose Yourself," especially if you saw his movie *8 Mile*, and Rachel Platten's "Fight Song." Regardless of the specific song, movie, book, poem, speech, TV show, person, or blog, I urge you to find and use often whatever you can to fire your belly, spark your heart, and help give your reasons to motivate you. It could be a list of your goals. It could be your whys. It could be the time you look at your spouse, your child, or yourself in the mirror and say that you deserve better! As you see different things, hear people, or have things happen to you, try to funnel each into a paradigm of inspiration. If your boss shows contempt for you and insinuates you are incompetent, try thinking, *That is a good reason to work toward my own business.*

Some of the other tactics I have seen, developed, or used include:

(1) If you are having trouble starting or committing for a long period, try at least five minutes. Often you will find some momentum and get a lot more done than five minutes' worth. Doing anything even for five minutes is better than nothing. Research a topic online, write down goals and ideas for how to achieve them. Do something and do it as often as you can, but in any event, good for you for doing something!

(2) Keep in mind that change can be tough, but staying the same can be tougher. Do you really want to stay the same? Isn't there a gnawing feeling inside that you should be doing more and doing better? Isn't it painful to be stuck and not moving toward your goals? Are the few minutes or hours of working on something you really want really that tough compared to enduring the status quo?

(3) Appreciate what you have and how far you have come. Each of the challenges you have faced have made you stronger and better able to deal with the next. The more you act and try, the better you become. Why not try right now. Consider giving yourself a reward for different milestones you meet. Give yourself something to work toward in the short term. Maybe set a goal of buying yourself that new coat, boots, or car until you hit a certain target goal. It could be something simple like doing an extra hour on your goal work today, and you will let yourself sleep in an extra hour on Saturday. Be careful to not give yourself counterproductive goals like a birthday cake to celebrate your losing ten pounds!

(4) Consider drawing and putting on the wall a progress chart. You can show your start point from a certain day, how far you have come, and how much longer until the next significant step is accomplished. Try not to overwhelm yourself with listing all of the steps and how far until your overall goal is met as being too far out. You can plan for when you get closer to completion, like you might book a hotel a week out for a trip, but concentrate on the things immediately in front of you: drive to the airport, find long-term parking, park, then go through baggage and get to the gate, each of which a necessary step. If you get frustrated along the way, remember how far you have come, and that should help motivate you to continue.

Commit your heart to your dream, your goal, and your desire, and your mind and body will follow! Figure out what steps you need to take, including the next step, and take it. Motivation does not mean you are having fun with what you are doing, but you could be! As I am writing these words, I am thinking again about hopefully making a positive difference in someone by sparking the right thought or emotion to spur them toward doing better. I suppose I may be a naïve fool, but it gives me a feeling of purpose to try. For what dream or goal might you be willing to risk being called naïve or a fool? Good for you if you have a dream big enough! Keep in mind, again, you don't have to. You get to!

Chapter Summary

- Inspiration and motivation drive action!
- There is always more inspiration and motivation to be found!
- Even when the spark of inspiration is low, move forward and act, and it will fan the flames!
- Find, fabricate, or spin inspiration and motivation!
- Dreaming, planning, and thinking about your dreams are great; now act!

Boost Your Willpower!

- Where there is a will there is a way!
- Use your willpower to guide your choices!
- Don't even think that giving up is an option!
- "People don't just find the strength and the willpower they need, they create it." —Anonymous
- You have untapped willpower, so use it!

During an online search about willpower, I found the following: from Merriam-Webster: "[26]The ability to control one's own actions, emotions, or urges, strong determination that allows one to do something difficult" and from another heading: "control exerted to do something or restrain impulses." And a third: "the ability to resist short-term temptation in order to reach long-term goals." Synonyms for willpower include: determination, resolve, drive, self-discipline, self-control, forbearance, nerve, fortitude and grit.

While often we think of willpower as the ability to avoid doing something wrong or bad for us, it is also the ability to move forward and make progress regardless of the obstacles we encounter. Another way to look at willpower is mental energy directed to a purpose. Willpower can keep you moving along when the glow of inspiration is distant and motivation seems to fade. You direct your will toward something, back it up with desire, and move it forward with the power of your actions.

Some articles I have read would lead you to believe that willpower is a limited resource and that it can run out. In this scenario, after being bombarded with multiple temptations, the thought is that anyone will eventually break down and give in (or give up). I suppose if your paradigm is such that all you ever see is the zero-sum game where you have to take to gain, then eventually willpower will break down. What if we prefer to see things from a different perspective, a perspective where after each temptation or test our character strengthens our resolve and makes us more resilient and confident? How about if the triggers we face that send us back to old bad habit could be turned into resolve pointers instead of triggers? What could we do with our willpower then?

Willpower is both self-imposed initiative and self-control. On one hand, we can feel a strong need to have or do something and chalk it up to "I couldn't help myself." On the other hand, if we don't feel a strong need to do something positive and don't get around to it, then "I didn't feel like it or at least not yet." If you struggle at times to bolster your willpower and find it lacking, you may need to use some tools to build it back up. Some of the tools that can help include:

(1) List or revisit your list of whys. Asking yourself what will you lose if you continue might help you to stop: "If I continue smoking, I may not live to see my daughter's wedding." Considering what will you gain might help you to act more: "If I continue to learn more and put in extra hours, I will have more opportunities and a better life."

(2) Some believe that willpower is like a muscle that can strengthen with exercise or atrophy with lack of use. With each exertion of your will by the choices you make, you are making something happen. Things in motion tend to stay in motion, while inaction breeds inaction. Do what you need to build confidence and momentum to continue. Keep in mind, it is not that you do not have willpower; at times, it is that you are not using it. Use your willpower some, and you will find it easier to use it more.

(3) Consider that willpower is exercising the control that you have over your own thoughts and actions. Since that is the case, isn't willpower the same thing as belief power? Maybe that is the problem at times. Maybe you don't believe that you can stop

doing something or that you lack initiative to do something new and stick with it. If so, who sold you that line of garbage? You are stronger than you know, and if you set your mind and your heart to something, your willpower will be there with you if you let it!

(4) Use your common sense when you can. If you know that you have certain things that trigger bad behavior, then avoid them. If you want to stay faithful to your spouse but know "how you get" sometimes when you are out drinking with the wrong crowd, just don't go drinking with the wrong crowd! If you want to get up an extra two hours early and get some goal work done and know that you tend to get up an hour later than you want, set the alarm for three hours early (sounds stupid but that is what I have been doing lately).

(5) Understand the processes that lead you to what you want. If you buy only healthy food at the supermarket, you won't have any unhealthy food around the house to tempt you. If you have one friend or set of friends that always tear down your dreams and aspirations, don't share with them. If you know when you are with a certain friend or two you always seem to engage in self-destructive behavior, limit your time with them. If you find that you always seem to have to try something new at least three times before you get it right, make sure you try at least three times!

Willpower doesn't have to be just about toughing it out in the short term so you can do better in the long term. It can be your mantra, your credo, what you have decided to do. It can help guide your decisions in the short term until they become habit. Commit yourself to following through with the actions you plan; start with one, move on to the next, and let it boost your sense of success. Do an extra five minutes' worth of exercise. Read an extra five pages. Make five more phone calls. All you have to do is decide to do them. That is the power of your will!

There is a common misconception out there that in order to be a success, you have to have the willpower to give up happiness in the short term to be happy in the long term. Sure, in order to do something meaningful you need to exert some effort, okay likely a lot of effort. But that does not mean that you have to be miserable while working toward your goals. It seems that when we look at others and see their successes there is a tendency for us to think: *They had it easy, they had all of the advantages, they were lucky, they enjoyed their work, and they had a drive and passion that I don't have.* If you have any of these thoughts, I have great news for you: you have access to all of the same advantages that really count, including enjoying your work and having drive and passion. The luck will follow. It is simple (I didn't say easy). You take the power of your will, convince yourself that you really want something, that you deserve it, that you can get it, that you will get it, start taking steps toward making that happen, and don't' give up! The rest is simply the mechanics of how, when, and working. You can enjoy the working, the progress, and yes even the setbacks if you decide that you want to. That is part of the awesomeness of your willpower!

You can use tools to keep you on track while you might not feel the desire or will to keep going. If you promise yourself you will do at least a certain amount at a specific time, you often will do that much, and more. Any amount of progress can be seen as a cause to feel good about your effort and keep you moving forward. Personally, I struggle with my willpower daily with getting my two hours of work done in the morning, doing only one hour in the morning then doing one in the evening. For each hour I miss on a weekday, I have to add an hour on the weekend in order for me to get my twenty hours in for the week (or at least close to it). I find myself unhappy at times with my lack of results but try to keep from becoming discouraged by concentrating on the fact that I am still making progress. While I know that I can do much better and will continue to do better, I try to give myself credit for success to date, which seems to encourage or motivate me to continue. The other thought that helps keep me working on things and trying to be productive is, *What else am I going to do right now?* I know that I should be doing something to move forward. If I don't, then how am I going to make things better and make progress?

I don't expect that you care whether I make any progress but what about you? Don't you deserve to do and be the best that you can for yourself, your family, your friends, and your future self? They say in business as stated earlier in this book, if you are not growing, you are dying. There is some wisdom in that for us to consider for ourselves. If we are not doing better, there is a tendency to backslide and do worse. Another way to think about willpower is that willpower is the engine that keeps you moving toward where you want to go. You can keep making progress and moving onward and upward if you have the engine of willpower. You need to add the fuel of desire, goals, planning, and effort. You have to navigate, assess how you are doing, and make course adjustments. When your boat's engine is broken, use the wind to push you. When there is no wind, use the oars. When you have no oars, paddle with your hands. If your boat sinks, swim!

I suppose to some people these ruminations and thoughts are childish and/or without merit. If we can expand how we look at things and consider them a different way, we can do more and better with what we have. With an initial thought, a desire can be born. From that desire can come great deeds, tremendous efforts, and wonderful things. A few words of encouragement can go a long way to supplant someone's willpower. I know that we don't necessarily, nor should we, need anyone else's support to hold to our own convictions and stick to our own plan, but a well-placed "good job" or "I am proud of you" is nice to hear at times, especially when you are at your lowest. I am not talking about some off-the-cuff comment from the background like Rob Schneider in an Adam Sandler movie with a random: "You can do it!" I mean real support like I got from my uncle after I made a real tough decision to break up with a long-time girlfriend and he said, "That must have taken a lot of guts." He didn't challenge me with, "Have you thought this through?" or "Are you sure?" Sometimes people in their attempt to support you can actually have the opposite effect by enabling you to be okay with less than your best. They can be too understanding of your short-comings and not hold you to a high standard. Maybe let you off with an "At least you gave it a good try!" Does any of that really help you, or does it minimize your need for good willpower to keep moving, trying, doing more, and doing better? Maybe you can benefit from a good coach who supports your goals, desires, efforts, milestones, and ability to stick to your planned actions and help you assess and do better. Nowadays, there are plenty of life coaches, business consultants, and others who can help you develop and stick to your plans. I tried working with a life coach for a while, and it helped me some for a time. To each their own. If you find something that works for you, use it but don't rely on it in case it is not always there.

Remember that your willpower is always there, even if you don't use it. How many times can you can be tested or tempted before your willpower fails? That is up to you. How strong is your will? How deep are your convictions? How deep is your desire? In most cases, you know what you need to do. It is in your power to do it. All you need to do is decide to do it. Decide to act. Decide to keep acting and doing for your goals, your reasons, your whys. It can be breaking a bad habit and stop doing something counterproductive or to start a new habit of being productive to accomplish your goals. Don't let your willpower ever be broken! You can have slips, failings, setbacks, disappointments, and temporary lapses, but never be broken! It is not about how many times you get knocked down; it is about getting back up each and every time! Don't expect perfection; give yourself a break when you lapse or relapse. But also don't let yourself off the hook too easily. Maybe do some extra to make up for the lapse. Learn from your failings and why they happened so you can be less likely to repeat them. I know that I already listed this at the beginning of this chapter, but it is so important to understand: "WHERE THERE IS A WILL THERE IS A WAY!"

Chapter Summary

- It is your will, your power, your willpower!
- You can rely on your willpower when your inspiration and motivation fade.
- You have an endless supply of willpower; you just need to use it!
- Set your mind to it and it will happen!
- You should strive for perfection, but cut yourself some slack if you have some setbacks!

Stop Procrastinating!

- "You cannot escape the responsibility of tomorrow by evading it today."—Abraham Lincoln
- Don't let procrastination rob you of your opportunities.
- Win the battle with yourself and act now!
- You owe it to your future self to do it now!
- Plan when to act and stick to your plan—for your sake!

While writing this book, I successfully faced down and defeated my long-time foe: procrastination. According to Merriam-Webster[27] online, the definition of procrastinate is: "to put off intentionally and habitually; to put off intentionally the doing of something that should be done." I guess that is a reasonable, politically correct, low-key, broad-stroke categorization for the term. I, on the other hand, have a little stronger definition: Procrastination is the insidious, treacherous, evil thief of dreams, goals, success, ambition, time, and opportunities that can rob beggar and king alike of life's wonders and meaningful content.

I don't think I worded that definition as strongly as I wanted to. How many times have you said someday you would like to do something but never do? How many times do you not get around to pursuing an ambition, dream, or goal? I took decades to finally get around to writing a book. In this chapter, I hope to share with you some of my insights and research into why we delay or put things off and what we can do to minimize this dream thief called procrastination. The good news is that the better you understand why you procrastinate and use proven tools to move past that wet blanket restricting you, the better you will do and the more successful you will be.

From my own experience and research, I understand many of the reasons we procrastinate.

The biggest culprit is probably fear. We have a natural fight-or-flight response to fear that raises our adrenalin, heightens our awareness, and increases our ability to cope with or avoid danger. It is an automatic response programmed into us to avoid harm and can save us from impending injury or death. That is not the type or level of fear that I am referring to as a contributor to procrastination. It is the types of fear that, based on what ifs, maybes, and worries, unnecessarily stop or impede us from doing what we should to achieve our goals. I found a list of the types of fears I am referring to posted online by fearlessliving.org[28]:

1. Fear of failure
2. Fear of loss
3. Fear of change
4. Fear if intimacy
5. Fear of being judged
6. Fear of success
7. Fear of the unknown
8. Fear of loneliness
9. Fear of rejection
10. Fear of not being good enough

Unlike the fight-or-flight call-to-action response to potential real harm, these fears are action-crippling inhibiting worries about what might happen and harm us versus help us. The good news is that we can go forward despite these fears, especially if we can minimize them knowing that they are based on maybes. We can control how we deal with each of our fears. It is not courage to have no fear. It is courage to act even though you have fear. Do you want to live in fear with no trying, no successes, no failing, and learning with no risk at all? Is that really living? Are any of the above fears real enough to give rise to that nasty procrastination of not getting started yet, or even worse, deciding to never start or try?

Another reason we might put off acting or moving forward is not knowing what we can or should do. In the Make it Real, Start Doing Better, and Steps for Doing Better chapters, I mention some tools to move forward, including setting goals and actions that you can do to accommodate them. The best plans and intentions to act will not get anything done in the long run. Yes, they are needed to define and describe what and when you want to do it, but without acting upon them, they are useless. Let us assume you have desire, a goal, and some plans and steps to take, and it is going to take a lot of work with some potential setbacks. You are inspired and motivated, but you feel that maybe you can start tomorrow or maybe after the holidays or when you have more time from work or maybe as soon as tomorrow.

Nothing is going to happen until you actually do it! Don't kid yourself. If you want to make progress, you have to take steps to do so. Things aren't going to just happen because you planned them or thought about them; you have to do them. So, if you struggle at times to get started or to get or stay on track, what are some of the things that you can do to stop procrastinating and get things done by starting now?

Mark Twain wrote: "Eat a live frog first thing in the morning and nothing worse will happen to you on that day." There is also a book by motivational speaker and writer Brian Tracy titled *Eat That Frog*. The premise of the book is that if you have to do something unappealing, do it first and get it out of the way. In other words, do the most difficult thing first, then the rest will seem easier. It is one of the ways to stop procrastinating by leaving the difficult things for a later time. I can only imagine what you might be thinking at this point, *WTF? What's the frog got to do with anything?* Okay, maybe it makes sense as a metaphor to eat the frog first as a good way to get started, and it might even help at times to think of difficult tasks in that way. I want to share with you some other ways that you might be able to get moving, get moving now, and keep moving and acting as often and as long as you need to in order to accomplish your goals.

From my research, experience, and current thoughts, I have the following tips, tactics, and suggestions for you to try to battle your own version of procrastination or inability to start and continue working on the things you need to so you can reach your goals. Use whatever works for you, and change up tactics if need be. We can be fickle beings, and what works for us today may not work tomorrow, but keep moving forward and try the following:

1. Set your targets and measure your progress.
2. Set more meaningful targets and behavior goals if your other ones are not working.
3. Wherever possible try to see the tasks that you need to complete as fun, meaningful things that you want to get done and you *want* to start. Remember, you don't *have* to do them. You *get* to do them and reach your goals!
4. While it is true that if you are going to do something, do it well; doing something poorly and making progress and learning from it is far better than doing nothing at all.
5. Inaction promotes inaction. Action promotes action. Oftentimes, the first step or act is the toughest because it is first, but once you get started it is easier to keep going.
6. Try to develop good habits of getting things done. Maybe you can set aside a certain time of day to work on important things.
7. Make a to-do list daily in whatever format works best for you:

- Microsoft To Do
- Outlook
- Simplenote
- Other apps or programs for your phone, computer, or tablet, possibly with a timer
- An old-school daily planner such as the Daytimer that I use
- A calendar
- Sticky tabs or Post-it Notes
- A simple piece of paper

8. Write down what you need to do and it becomes more real, especially if you include a time when you plan to do it. You will also be less likely to forget to do things if they are written down.
9. Plan to give yourself rewards for tasks done or milestones met.
10. Commit to doing at least five minutes to get started, then see if you want to continue.
11. Tell someone supportive that you plan to get something done and when you plan to do it.
12. Do what you need to do and what works for you. For example, I often sleep later than I planned to and don't get as much done because of it, so I set the alarm a half hour or hour earlier. I know how lame that sounds, but it works for me.
13. Use your motivation and inspiration tools and tactics to push you past inaction and procrastination and do something now!
14. Stop doing the busy work of filing and organizing and actually do something meaningful.
15. Be your own worst critic when you delay or postpone doing something. Be your biggest supporter and appreciate your progress when you do something.
16. Say no to distractions and meaningless tasks.
17. If you have an inbox, clear it daily!
18. Just because you did something today doesn't mean you should start putting things off again tomorrow. Don't let yourself backslide into old habits or ruts.
19. Don't waste time handling things more than once. Do something start to finish when appropriate, which will free you up for the next tasks.
20. Try to get better daily in what you do and how you do it, and it will be easier to start again the next day.
21. Stop making excuses for why you can't do something, and list ways of how you can do it.
22. Try to do something worth bragging about to yourself, and let it motivate you to continue.

23. Keep your workplace organized so you don't get slowed down with spending time finding things as another reason to procrastinate.
24. Break your goals into reasonable steps, and commit to the actions you need to do for the first step, including when you are going to do them.
25. Turn off your social networks and set aside or shut off your phone so you can focus and get things done.
26. Pick one big thing to work on as a minimum each day.
27. Have a contingency plan for when your schedule goes awry.
28. Make sure that your to-do lists are realistic and doable in the time you allowed for them.
29. If you miss a goal or otherwise disappoint yourself, don't double over with guilt and remorse; double down on committing to do better.
30. If you get stuck, switch to a different task, but don't stop making progress.
31. Be the warrior you know you can be, and fight through your inaction one step and one battle at a time.
32. Refuse to consider yourself a victim of circumstance or disadvantaged. There are many with less who have excelled. You are not too old, too young, or otherwise inhibited from acting now and doing better!
33. Appreciate what you have, including the wonderful opportunities in front of you, and take steps toward them.
34. Do you really think you will do something tomorrow if you are unwilling to do it today?
35. If you are worried about the risk of trying and failing, balance that against the risk of never succeeding by doing nothing.
36. Continuously adjust your tactics to your circumstances, and do what works for you and when as you need to. Remember your biggest foe, you, knows you best!

37. If procrastination is a habit for you, treat it as such and make a plan to break it. First, admit that you have an issue with it. Second, decide you want to stop. Use all of the tactics you can to stop, including the most powerful one, action!
38. If you are really never going to do something, come to grips with it and move on to something you will do.
39. Do one thing at a time. Do it well. Do it now.
40. Use that awesome power of choice, and choose to act now!

Remember, you have the ultimate tool to combat procrastination. You have the power of choice! It is simple. Choose to act and do what is needed. I did not say it was easy, but it is that simple! When it comes down to it, why wouldn't you just do what you need to do or at least try? Is it fear? Don't you deserve at least to try? Action defeats fear. Progress promotes confidence. Confidence helps maintain motivation. Motivation promotes action!

Chapter Summary

- One of the main reasons we procrastinate is fear.
- Bravery is not acting without fear; it is acting despite fear!
- Use whatever tactics and tools you can to defeat that nasty enemy of success we know as procrastination!
- If you don't do it now, will you really do it tomorrow?
- Choose your destiny; choose to and act now!

Using Your Gifts to Do Better in Your Roles

- "Often what we do speaks louder than who we are." —Abraham Lincoln
- Don't you want to look back and say, "Well done!"?
- You can provide the spark to ignite greatness!
- Don't you always deserve better?
- How many ways can you do better?

Put some thought into what your gifts are. In what areas do you excel? I have been told that I have the gift of encouragement. Knowing that is a big part of my inspiration to write this book. One way to identify your gifts and talents is to think about what things that you enjoy doing. While there are some people who really enjoy singing, sometimes they are not as good as they think. In most cases, though, people enjoy doing what they do well and do well in what they enjoy doing.

What is your heart song? What drives you? If you could do anything in life, what would it be? If you had some encouragement earlier in life, would you be better today? You still have a lot left to do and to give. If you knew back then what you know now, how much further along to your dreams and goals would you be? Instead of feeling less when you see others succeed, why not offer some assistance when you can and revel in their accomplishments knowing you helped in some way?

What are your talents and gifts? For a list of some of the talents and gifts people have, see Appendix 1.

I have gathered from different lists available on the internet, added some, and deleted some.

If you want to do better and be better, put some thought into what your roles are. Many of our common roles include:

parent	employee	employer	athlete	service provider
teacher	student	leader	partner	family member
spouse	friend	companion	customer	patient
boyfriend	girlfriend	negotiator	salesperson	administrator
assistant	director	neighbor	performer	critic
mentor	guide	coach	example	motivator
advisor	caregiver	counselor	entertainer	negotiator
author	builder	politician	reporter	society member

I will also include one of the best roles we can have: hero!

We all find ourselves in some of the above roles at different times. If you want to do better, what does that mean? Do better at what? We have hopefully determined why we want to do better—ultimately to achieve our goals and be successful. Think about the roles listed above and the fact that many of us might find ourselves in half of them at any given time.

They say that there are more positions possible in chess (10 to the power of 120) than there are atoms in the visible universe (10 to the power of 88). That means number 1 with 120 zeros after it versus the number 1 with 88 zeros after it. Huge numbers in either case. Assuming for each of the above roles, there are at least ten areas we can identify to work on to get better at doing each role. There are forty roles listed, and maybe we each engage in half, which is twenty with ten areas in each to work on. That would be two hundred areas for us to work on. Add to that the number and combination of talents we can apply, and I have no idea how many different combinations of roles, areas, and talents for us to work on there are. In any event, there is plenty for us to do. But it is way too much for any of us to consider working on at the same time. I suggest you consider picking three of the most important roles that you want to improve.

After picking three roles that you want to be better at doing, try to list ten things that you can do better in each. If you need some help with coming up with ways to do better in each, try looking it up online. Pick the top three things you can do better in each. Set daily and/or weekly goals to do for each. Try to stick to your behavior goals for at least three weeks, after which they are likely to become habits.

For example, the roles in which I want to do better are as follows: spouse (husband), author, and motivator.

Things to Do to Be a Better

Husband

1. Leave daily "I love you" and reason why notes.
2. Dedicate at least two hours per weekend to "honey-do" items around the house.
3. Give at least one compliment per day.
4. Ask my wife more regularly what would make her happier.
5. Give her a massage once per week.
6. Spend at least two hours per week helping with her business.
7. Share with her more on a daily basis how my workday went.
8. Start a weekly date-night surprise on a certain day as a tradition.
9. Find a new store she would like per week and visit it with her.
10. Take the dog out for at least one extra time per day so she doesn't have to.

Author

1. Include who said it each time I list a quote.
2. Continue writing if time allows each week, even past the twenty-five-hundred-word target.

3. Review work to date monthly for content and context.
4. Find an editor to review manuscript when done for grammar and content.
5. Research what the audience/beneficiary group is.
6. Accept that first drafts are often bad and have to be revised.
7. Read aloud what I have written and consider changing.
8. Eliminate unnecessary words from my writing.
9. Ask, "What would my hero write when reviewing or starting to write?"
10. Research and implement tips to be a better writer.

Four items in this list were taken from online lists of how to be a better writer.

Motivator

1. Research and show some information about the speaker when showing a quote.
2. Continue to read motivational and inspirational books and learn.
3. Continue with telling people they are doing a good job—at least one per day.
4. Make sure to use "you could" versus "you should" in talking and writing.
5. Use more inspirational stories in daily conversation and writing.
6. Smile more (for some reason difficult for me).
7. Be more empathetic.
8. Mention to others things that I admire about them.
9. Be more outwardly enthusiastic, which can be contagious.
10. Say to at least one person each day, "Today will be an awesome day."

For each of the categories above, I have chosen to implement it in the near future or concentrate on being better at it.

Husband

1. Leave daily "I love you" and reason why notes.
2. Ask my wife more regularly what would make her happier.
3. Share with her more on a daily basis how my workday went.

Author

1. Continue writing if time allows each week, even past the twenty-five-hundred-word target.
2. Research what the audience/beneficiary group is and their typical goals.
3. Research and implement tips to be a better writer.

Motivator

1. Continue to read motivational and inspirational books and learn.
2. Use more inspirational stories in daily conversation and writing.
3. Say to at least one person each day, "Today will be an awesome day."

If you decide to go through this exercise, I expect you will find it harder than you think. I have been working on trying to do so for many years, but until writing this book, I had not formulated this approach. I found it much more difficult than I thought it would be. I also feel better about having gone through the exercise than I expected. It would have been much easier for me to just list anything if I were not trying to honestly do better myself, be an example to you, and just offer to you a tool for doing better.

In any event, the general idea is that if you want to do better and be better, you need to define what that means and identify how you can make that happen. It has always been true that learning wisdom from others' sometimes painful experiences is much easier than learning wisdom from your own painful experiences. In the past twenty years or so, the internet has made it so much easier to find information.

You no longer have to go to a library, buy a book (although I suggest you do that too), buy an audio or video program, or attend seminars or lectures. Now you can just type in what you want to learn about, find all kinds of information, read it right away, and/or save it for later reading and review.

At this point, hopefully you have identified your dreams. You have set time frames and specified the dreams into goals. You have broken your goals into steps that you can attain and manage. You have identified roles in which you want to do better. You have specified three areas or so of each role where you want to get better. Having your goals and plans is a great start. The fact that you have goals puts you far above most people with at best have only dreams, too afraid to take the responsibility of having goals. Now you know what you want to do. Good for you! Do you feel like you are doing better already? Now what?

Now you start doing. You do what you planned to do (or more). I suggest you keep a list of things you do or check off on your to-do list the things you get done. Expect that you are going to have some failures, which is how we learn. Feel free to share with supportive friends or family your goals and steps you plan to do when you accomplish them. Be careful of those who want to tear you down, point out the downsides or risks, and belittle your dreams. Under the guise of "just wanting to be helpful," they are showing their fear that you will succeed and they will feel less successful. After you reach your goals, feel free to brag a little about what you accomplished and the progress you have made.

Sometimes I set behavior goal-accomplishing reward bonuses for myself. The bonuses I use may be minor, such as when I wanted to reach 20,000 words written for this book draft, after which I would take a break, lay on the couch, and maybe catch a quick nap for an hour. At the time of this writing (a Saturday), I was at 19,981 words. I was about sixteen and a half hours into my project time weekly goal (the week ends for my weekly goal on Sunday 11:59 p.m.). I had just made it to 20,009 words and then took my break.

Chapter Summary

- What roles do you have?
- What does doing better look like to you?
- How can you best use your gifts and talents in your roles?
- Think of the benefit you can be to others as you do better.
- Acknowledge and feel good when you do better.

Helping Others in Your Roles

- You can be the light in someone's darkness.
- Encouragement is free.
- The world misses out when you are not doing your best.
- You count more than you know.
- What you do makes a difference!

Remember: you are here on earth to do great things! I am not sure if it's when you do better you become better, or if when you become better you do better. In any case, they seem to go hand in hand. If you can find tactics, methods, and ways to do better at your roles and goals, you will do better and be better at doing them. As you do better, you will feel better. When you feel better you will do better. From each failure, you learn to do better. From each skill and the knowledge you acquire, you become better. When you help more people, you do better with more rewards. Your value increases and you become better. Do better with a simple thing: be a bright spot in someone's day with a compliment and you become better. It doesn't have to come from a specific role you have or your job per se; you can do better for better's sake and in turn be better yourself.

When I was going for radiation treatments each day for five weeks, my mom and I would wait in the waiting room of the radiation oncology treatment area of the big teaching hospital. It was not a real uplifting area with the typical seats, magazines, and institutional look and feel. There was a banner up on the wall that read: "Has anyone told you today that you're terrific?" Since the first day we saw that, I would ask my mom every day at the hospital, "Has anyone told you today that you're terrific, Ma?"

She answered each time, "No, Mark."

And I would respond with, "You're terrific, Ma."

She would respond with, "Thank you, Mark."

It doesn't sound like a big thing, but for the next twenty-seven years, whenever my mom was having a tough time, or often just out of the blue, I would ask her the same: "Has anyone told you today that you're terrific, Ma?"

She answered each time, "No, Mark."

And I would respond with, "You're terrific, Ma."

Then she would thank me and tell me I am a good son. Through my mom's two-year struggle with the liver cancer from which she died, I would ask her the same, this time with her as the patient, and she would answer the same.

I don't know if anyone else ever got so much from that banner in the waiting room, but we sure got a lot of mileage and solace from it. Thank you so much for whoever put it there. You never know how much impact you might have with what you do, say, or write. Think of how much good you can do with your actions. You will be compensated in many ways. Set your mind toward your goals and doing better, work hard, and you will meet or exceed your expectations. Learn from others how to do better and be better. Later in the book, there are a lot of quotes and pearls of wisdom that I hope will help you do better and be better. For now, if you can hear me, Ma: "Has anyone told you today that you're terrific? You're terrific, Ma!"

You never know what an impact a few words of encouragement, gratitude, or other communication or deed will have. You can definitely make someone's day or have a lifetime impact. School teachers often know they have the awesome ability to not only teach information but to inspire short-term and long-term success.

What are some of the things that you can do that might help others and at the same time help yourself be better and feel confident that that you can and are doing good and better? I challenge you to take a good look inside of yourself; be honest and try to think of what are your three biggest and best talents or gifts. Even if right now you don't feel or think that you are very talented, we all can think of at least three things that we are better at doing than other things.

For me, my top three talents are encouraging, problem-solving, and coping well. If you are struggling with what talents or gifts you might have, take a look at the list shown in Appendix 2. I have been told that I have the gift of encouragement. I have also had some good feedback by some of the people I have encouraged in the past. As part of my education in engineering, we learned to take math, science, and other available data to create solutions to problems. As far as coping goes, I know that I can get through anything no matter how difficult or intense of a situation. Let's face it; you can too. We have no choice but to cope. We either cope well or poorly. While it is later in life that I developed the right combination of goal setting, planning, self-discipline, and commitment to start making my dreams a reality, I am glad I have finally done so and am making good progress. I was reading the other day in Napoleon Hill's book *Think and Grow Rich* that he was of the mindset that most successful people don't start excelling until they reach their forties or fifties. I keep in mind that he wrote this book around 1930 and expect that by now our fifties are the new forties, and I am only fifty-four years old. This is not to say that I had no successes earlier in life, but my dreams and big important goals are starting to take form, and I am now making good progress toward them. It does not matter how old you are; you can still make your dreams happen! The side benefit is that you will be doing better and being better as you make progress.

When you look at your top talents or gifts, what does that tell you about how you can best be of benefit to others and be a success? What specific benefits do you have to offer society with your talents? How great will it be when you are at the top of your field or profession? How will you do better and be better with your talents and gifts? If you have difficulty thinking of work, services, and vocations associated with your talents and gifts, you might do some research online that could give you some guidance.

You could always start your own business. If you can provide what people want, you will be successful. There is an old saying: "If you build a better mousetrap, the world will beat a path to your door." What is it you think you can do, or do better, that will benefit others or benefit them better? Each of us has the potential for greatness. I don't know you, your challenges, your difficulties, your talents, your gifts, your past, or your future.

One of the recurring themes I find in reading books and quotes from successful people is that if you desire something enough and work hard enough for it you can get it or something close to it. You may want to be a basketball or football star but lack the body in order to be one. You can, however, learn as much about the sport, work hard on researching, and become a foremost expert on coaching, sports commentating, have a blog following, or help people pick the best teams to wager on. You may also be able to mentor an aspiring person to excel and be successful in knowing you helped their achievements.

You are the master of your own destiny. That fact can scare you with the awesome responsibility that it puts on you or it can embolden you with the tremendous power that it gives you over your life. If you don't have a purpose, goal, or aim in life, all you have to do is pick one. Make a choice. While your dreams and goals may take a lot of work to achieve, think of how much sweeter the rewards will be knowing how much work you put into it. You may think at times, *Yeah, all this "you can do" stuff is for the go-getter, self-motivated, early riser, naturally ambitious types.* Not true! After decades of wanting to write a book that helps others, I finally succeeded. Even now, it is a daily struggle for me to put time into writing and other things I want to get done.

I have a forty-hour-per-week job as a construction project manager and travel weekdays forty-five miles each way to get there. This morning I hoped to get up two hours before normal to write but only got up one hour early. That leaves me another hour to write when I get home if I want to meet the weekly goals I set.

This past weekend on Sunday—the last day of my week in which I want to get at least twenty hours of "project work" done, including writing—I still had five hours to do things. There are times when I feel overwhelmed with all the things that I have to do. It helps me a lot to remember and frame the paradigm that it is all these things I "get to" do versus "have to" do. I remember all too well how it felt when I was unemployed and looking for a job for five months or so. The bills don't stop coming. I had the feeling of being a failure daily and weekly with trying to get a new job. I don't have to go to work today, I get to!

I also remember many times over the years wanting to be very successful at something, to make a difference, to help people, and to have a greater purpose than just getting by. Maybe at some point I wanted to be a big-shot, star, or otherwise "big-noise." After too many years of minor successes here and there mixed in with a bunch of get by and some failures, I am now on track. It feels great and meaningful and helps dispel fear of failure and the tendency for self-criticism to know that I am making progress. Another recurrent theme from books and sayings I come across is the power of action. All the plans, goals, preparations, and hopes are meaningless without action. Action brings results. Results bring progress. Progress brings success.

When I went out on my own with my own consulting business it felt like I was jumping off a cliff with a bag and hoped the bag had a parachute. I actually did well for a while, then just kind of got by, then didn't do too well, then went back to work for other people. I did learn a lot about self-reliance. Unfortunately, I did not grow with hiring other employees and growing business networks as I should have. I suppose if I knew how to access my will power and self-discipline back then, I would have done much better. Maybe it wasn't the right time, and I wasn't ready. I feel good that I tried something on my own and took a risk. I am doing better now and every day making progress on my dreams and goals. The only real risks I am taking right now is putting all this time, effort, and some minimal money into dreams and goals for my wife and me. Other risks, such as feeling like a failure at times, feeling like a fool for trying, and not succeeding, I can accept. None of them are real, if I don't let them be, and I have decided to put the time in. The time will pass anyway, even If I don't do the work.

How many new things would you try if you weren't afraid? How many more risks would you take if you knew that even if you fail, you can try again or try something else? What new chances would you take if they were exciting and worth taking? How much better would you feel about yourself knowing you threw your heart into doing the best that you can? What if the opportunities for you to be truly successful and happy were all around you? Well, let me share with you the great news! The opportunities are there. You can be extremely happy and successful. There is only one person stopping you. Go look in the mirror. When you do, say enough! I can succeed! I will succeed! And I will make it happen!

Chapter Summary

- What you do matters, often in ways you don't know about.
- Do better and you can have great impacts.
- When you do better, you are becoming better.
- Do the actions, create results, make progress, and succeed.
- Decide to make your goals happen and they will!

Doing Something to Move Forward

- You are the master of your own destiny.
- Do it, do it now, do it better!
- What else are you going to do?
- You get to do anything you want, including nothing.
- Don't you want to do something?

If you have your goals written, set an appointment with yourself to spend at least one hour per day on doing things to move you forward. If it is easier, do two half-hour sessions if need be or four fifteen-minute sessions. Do something. If you don't know what you can or should do, consider doing one or more of the following:

1. Collect and review research online about what you want to do (you can save the info in a computer file maybe named "Goal Research." If the file is not in a format you can save, maybe try to highlight the info, copy it, and paste it to a Word document that you can save or print it to a PDF).
2. Spend some time brainstorming ideas of things you can do and write them down.
3. Find and buy books about your goal area (many used books online cost three to six dollars each, including delivery).
4. Write a mission statement or vision statement.
5. Look up ideas for: new businesses, home-based business, businesses by talents/gifts.

6. Call and set up a brainstorming session with a supportive friend or family member about things you can do.
7. Email, text, or message someone you think would have good ideas and be supportive, and ask them.
8. Write a list of some behavior goals (phone calls, emails, web sites searched, meetings with people, etc.).
9. Visualize and/or draw a picture or sketch of you reaching your goal.

I understand the natural reluctance to do something new, and I understand the tendency to procrastinate and put off until a later date. Over the past couple of months, I have developed a new tool to help motivate me to get things done. I have even had some success with suggesting it to others. Last week I visited an office building where we had done some work and needed to address an apparent water leak. While I was there, I asked a woman working there if she was all ready for Thanksgiving—we were about a week prior. She said that she had to cook for so many—there is so much she has to do and so much work. I told her that I had recently found a better way to think of things in a similar situation that was helping me. I said, "Think about how you 'get to do' all of those tasks, not you 'have to.'"

She paused briefly and said, "Thank you. That helps."

I suggest that as you think about all the things you "have to do" to achieve your goals and dreams, they are really things that you "get to do."

What if some of the ideas presented in this book—dreams, goals, things to do—sound good, maybe someday would be nice, but "that's not me" to you. If you have made it through my writing to this point, you must be extremely bored with absolutely nothing else to do, or maybe there are at least a few things you might want to do better. There must be some spark of hope and/or desire for you to do better. Maybe you are not ready to have good things happen yet, or to feel better about yourself by making some good steps with positive actions. Do yourself some good and at least fake it for a while. Don't you deserve at least that? If at some point you might care about achieving some goals or doing some things, what would they be? Write them down. Commit to faking it, if necessary, spend thirty minutes today writing down some goals and what about them you would enjoy or how they would otherwise be good to achieve. Commit also to spending some time each day researching and writing down how you might accomplish your goals and things that you can do to achieve them and taking steps to achieve them. Do this for at least three weeks. Put a note on your refrigerator to remind you to work on your goals every day. Make a mark on that note or another sheet to document what you worked on each day. Eventually, as you make some progress, you will believe more in what you are doing and hopefully feel motivated to continue.

Even if you are on track with your goals and making some good progress, make sure you smile when you have the chance, even if you don't want to. Be positive whenever you can. Point out the good you see in people, even if you are not feeling great yourself. I expect, more often than not, as you push yourself to do one good thing after another you might even convince yourself that you do good things and can do and be better. In any event, you will be doing better and being better in the process. Your progress and attitude will be self-perpetuating and contagious to others.

I have read some books, listened to some programs, and attended some seminars and training that have specific systems or steps to follow in order to be successful. I don't think that one is better than the other. I expect that some approaches work for some people and other approaches for others. Some type of specific steps and actions and interim goals help us through the times when inspiration and motivation waiver and lag. Find whatever works for you and keeps you on track. Isn't it exciting to know how much power you have to change what you do, how you do it, and do better? Do it! Do it now! Do it daily!

Ideas for Doing Better

Along with the ideas shared earlier in this book, I want to offer to you some other tips and tactics for doing better that I have come across. I expect that some you already know and use, some you have heard before, and some might be new. Hopefully you find some of them useful tools you can implement and make it possible for you to do even better:

1. Admit when you make a mistake.
2. Forgive others their mistakes.
3. Forgive your own mistakes.
4. Take one for the team when appropriate.
5. Take responsibility and the power that comes with it.
6. Disagree better: try "yes and ..." instead of immediately opposing.
7. Admit when you don't know something.
8. Follow up appropriately to "I don't know" with "but I can find out."
9. Help better: ask, "How can I help you with that?" or "With what can I help you?"
10. Be present for discussions, stop looking elsewhere, and make eye contact.
11. Praise loudly, correct softly.
12. Speak up when you see injustice.
13. Go on impressions, not assumptions.
14. Be the voice of reason in a petty dispute.
15. Pick up litter when you walk by even if it isn't yours.
16. Be stubborn about your ends but flexible about your means.
17. Sometimes someone close to you just needs a hug.
18. Try not to tell people they are wrong—offer alternatives.
19. Be the bright spot in someone's day.
20. Let the other person do most of the talking.
21. Be an active listener.
22. Do good things even when no one is looking.

23. Think from the other person's point of view.
24. Commit to doing better.
25. Always be learning.
26. Be slow to anger.
27. Own and continuously maintain your attitude.
28. Be polite always.
29. Do the hardest thing first.
30. Boost the self-esteem of others.
31. Be an owner of your situation, not a victim.
32. Keep all your promises.
33. Lead with enthusiasm.
34. Stay optimistic.
35. Encourage people to learn.
36. Keep learning always.
37. Don't criticize others.
38. Learn from past mistakes.
39. Appreciate the here and now.
40. Do good deeds and random acts of kindness.

The tactics shown are from the experiences and recommendations of successful people over their lifetimes, wisdom carried through the ages, and recurring themes in ancient to modern texts, all presented for you to use to do better and be better. You can also find other knowledge and wisdom at your fingertips on the internet. You can do a lot of things daily to do better, one thing once in a while, or go back and forth sometimes doing more, sometimes doing less. Again, you don't have to. You get to!

The other day I was out with my father and we stopped at a coffee shop that we visit weekly. It is not a very busy place, so there are not that may different people who work there. Usually, we are served by one of two women. One woman tends to have a poor attitude, say that some things are not available when they likely are, and almost never smiles.

The other is always eager to help, calls my dad sweetie or honey, always able to provide what we want or offer a similar alternative, and smiles often. When we were there the other day, we had the eager, pleasant, helpful woman serve us. I told her that she had a great attitude and that she was our favorite worker at the place. She gave me a beaming smile and said that I made her day. I felt great at the time for making her day and feel good about it now. My current goal is to find a way to highlight something the not-so-friendly worker does well, thank her appropriately, and see if I can't help her improve her attitude. From a service staff person to a coworker, friend, spouse, child, or other contact, what can you say or how can you help be the bright spot in their day?

If you want to do better daily and are looking for some ideas of good things you can do or simple ways to do better by doing some good deeds, take a look at Appendix 2. This list of good deed ideas comes from lists I found on the internet plus some additional ones from me. You don't need to be a saint, a martyr, or an altruist to do good deeds, especially the ones that don't cost you significant time or money. The next time someone tells you about an idea, goal, or dream they have, maybe pause for a moment and instead of pointing out potential risks or downsides, maybe give some encouragement, say, "That sounds exciting!" or "Great idea!"

Falling Off the Wagon

There is a term now most commonly used to describe recovering alcoholics or addicts who go back to their old bad habits as "falling off the wagon." A Salvation Army officer once told me that back in the late 1800s, the Salvation Army used to go around a city with a horse-drawn wagon, pick up street drunks, and bring them to a rehabilitation center or church for treatment to stop drinking. When they would go back to drinking, it was referred to as "falling off the wagon." I did a recent internet search that said that the daughter of William Booth, founder of the Salvation Army, Evangaline Booth, born 1865—the same year her father founded the organization—used to drive a wagon though the Bowery Slums in New York City to bring them to get help with sobriety. As a side note, I also found a competing definition for "falling off the wagon" of dirty water falling off of some water wagon, which I think someone made up—be careful of information from an internet search.

I recently felt that I was "off the wagon" when in the past few weeks I backslid into not waking up early to work on goals, not working in the evening, and not meeting my weekly goal of twenty hours per week. I had a few weeks where I only got seventeen or eighteen hours in, including weekends, but the last few weeks I got only seven to eleven hours each in, with no good reason other than extra sleep and some extra TV time. I know it doesn't sound like much, but I have been doing so well the past five months, and I woke up this morning after a couple of days of doing nothing on goals and felt like I was back to my old habit of procrastinating. I am not sure if subconsciously I am afraid as I get closer to some big milestones or thoughts like *Who do you think you are to think you can benefit a lot of people?* How am I dealing with it? For the first time in a few weekdays, I actually got up an hour early, making some progress, and it feels good to do so. I am going to feel good that I got at least seven to eleven hours in instead of feeling like I "fell off the wagon" and slept in a few days. The point I am trying to make is that if you find yourself backsliding, doing some of the same old bad habits, or not doing as well as you know you can, give yourself a break. You know that you can do better. Learn from your insight, frame the paradigm as a growth experience, move on, and do better! You are reading this book, so apparently, I got past some trials with "falling off the wagon" and you can too!

Some Grammar Tips

I will share a few suggestions on how you can use words and grammar more effectively.

When you speak or write, or at least if you are trying to correct someone's speech, try to get it right so that you don't look too wrong yourself. It seems in today's increasingly politically correct and woke society the attempt to sound superior with the use if *I* instead of *me* is laughably used improperly by the pompous overcritical and the innocents just wanting to sound correct. It has actually become so prevalent that you see it done on the news and by otherwise well-spoken, educated people.

I and *me* are both pronouns that we use to refer to ourselves. Use *I* when it is the subject of the verb (I will do that) or (I went somewhere) and use "me" when it is the object of the verb (he gave it to me) or follows a preposition (she went above me).

The difficulty that people seem to have is when there is more than one object in a sentence, and one is me. They correctly make sure the first-person subject is second to the first—she and I, or Susan and I, went somewhere or did something—as the subject. But when it comes to multiple objects, yes, the first-person subject comes second—the teacher scolded Susan and me—but is changed to *me* instead of *I*.

To double-check which to use and when, take the non-first-person subject or object out of the sentence. You would not say, "Me went somewhere or did something." You would use *I*. You also would not say the teacher scolded I; you would say the teacher scolded me.

Sometimes people try to sound smart or sophisticated with the word *utilize* instead of *use*. I used to think it was just a matter of both words meaning the same thing, with one being more pompous and longer. I just looked it up online, and it is worse than that.

Apparently, *utilize* means put into service for an otherwise not intended application[29]. The example I saw was "I use my frying pan to cook with, but I have utilized it as a weapon." So, you may not only sound pompous if you say *utilize* instead of *use* but also be wrong and sound uneducated. If you want to impress someone with your command of grammar, don't say, "You and me should utilize the best grammar rules that have been explained to us."

For those of you prone to saying "to be honest with you …" or "to tell you the truth …," does that mean that other times you are not being honest or telling the truth? Maybe try saying: "to be candid with you…." or "to be open with you …," which is what you probably mean and doesn't raise a red flag about your honesty or truth-telling.

Keep in mind also that all our spoken and written communication with words is "verbal." If you want to make a distinction that something is spoken, not written, then it is "oral." You will note on the TV shows and movies about court trials that the spoken arguments are "oral arguments."

When you do find that you want to help someone with their grammar, try to be helpful versus tear them down by pointing them out as wrong. As much as you might want to correct the pompous-sounding wrong person, it probably won't help, as they are likely to argue with you and argue that they are correct. I know this from experience because this exact thing has happened to me a few times. Maybe next time I will remember to handle it better with a "have you thought maybe that might not be the best way to say that?" or something like that. Bear with me; I have my own issues.

Chapter Summary

- Brainstorm, make lists, and plan to do things.
- Do something, and keep doing it on a regular basis.
- Commit to doing better daily where you can.
- Give yourself a break when you "fall off the wagon" and get back on track.
- Communicate better, and help others to do so as well.

Additional Inspiration and Wisdom from Others

- You freely use things developed by others, such as a car and a smartphone, so why not use theories and methods by others to achieve your goals?
- Ride the trails blazed by others by learning from them!
- How much better can you do knowing that many have done similar to what you want to do?
- Let the wind of others' successes fill your sails!
- Learn from the hardships of others and save yourself the trouble.

As you are going along making progress each day, try to learn as you go. When you make mistakes, learn from them. Try not to make the same mistakes more than once. On the other hand, when you do something well and succeed, make a note so you can repeat it in the future and share with others if you want. This section of the book is designed to share with your knowledge, wisdom, quotes, and sayings to help you succeed.

As I continue to read books about how to do better and how to be better, I am amazed at how much I can still learn. I also see that there are many recurrent themes, methods, and tactics that others have used to be successful.

Again, we have the awesome access to information today that gives us access to knowledge and wisdom from so many who been successful and helped so many. Within a matter of minutes, you can find hundreds if not thousands of quotes from people about wisdom, motivation, doing better, and being better. To give you some validity to the following quotes, I have included some biographical info about each author. I expect you might want to know a little about their background before assuming any importance of what they said. Some of these people you may not have heard of but in their day were renowned successes in their fields, with a lot of hard-earned wisdom to share. I feel to some degree like I am disrespecting them by trying to boil down their lives and accomplishments to a few sentences, but I guess it is better than nothing. If any of the following seem to especially resonate with you, I encourage you to read more about them and their contributions to the world.

I have tried to include the best for you of the recent twenty-five books, including about five thousand pages, the lists of successful famous people, quotes, and ancient proverbs from the internet and the dozens of audio programs and books from my past. I expect you may have heard some before. As you read each, consider how they apply to you; highlight or write a list of those you think are most important, and try to incorporate them into your behavior and habits. Maybe you can write down some of your own as you continue to learn and share them with others in the future.

The quotes and who said them are listed in the order that I found them, copied them, or happened to remember them:

(1) "Success is not the key to happiness. Happiness is the key to success. If you love what you are doing you will be successful." —Albert Schweitzer

1875–1965: Albert Schweitzer, became a doctor and received the Nobel Peace Prize in 1952 for his humanitarian work in developing countries in Africa. He helped natives and attracted volunteers from all over the world. At the time he was one of the best-known people in the world as a pioneer helping people with no regard to ideology, nation, or religion (from Encyclopedia.com)[30].

(2) "Most of the important things in the world have been accomplished by people who have kept on trying while there is no hope."—Dale Carnegie

1888–1955: Dale Carnegie was born into poverty on a farm in Missouri. He was a salesman, actor, public speaker, and author of *How To Win Friends and Influence People*. He founded the Carnegie Institute with a national following. He helped people be better and do better not only across the United States but also internationally (Brittanica.com)[31].

(3) "A second of help is better than hours of advice."—Tamil proverb

The Tamil people are a culture of people primarily from southern India and southern Asia who have been around since 300 BC, with a history of early poetry and writings. I guess that a newer version of the saying might be Nike's "Just Do It!" when it comes to helping people (Wikipedia).

(4) "I find that the harder I work, the more luck I have."—Thomas Jefferson

1743–1826: Tomas Jefferson, the third president of the United States, wrote the Declaration of Independence, the words and ideas within, which have impacted human rights around the world. Jefferson was also a champion of religious freedom (Monticello.org)[32].

(5) "Motivation is what gets you started. Habit is what keeps you going."—Jim Rohn

1930–2009: Jim Rohn was successful businessman with success in direct selling. He was a talented speaker seminar leader. He was also the mentor of Mark R. Hughes, the founder of Herbalife and Tony Robbins the self-help author and motivational speaker (Wikipedia)[33].

(6) "A goal is not always meant to be achieved; it often serves as something to aim at."—Bruce Lee

1940–1973: Bruce Lee is known as one of the best martial artists ever. He was a film and television actor and producer known for extreme training and self-discipline. He was an instructor of martial arts and philosopher (Wikipedia)[34].

(7) "Whatever the mind can conceive it can achieve."—Napoleon Hill

Oliver Napoleon Hill (1883–1970) wrote one of the ten best-selling self-help books of all time: *Think and Grow Rich*. He studied and interviewed over five hundred successful people over twenty years, collecting research and insights into how and why people succeed. He was a firm believer in visualizing and concentrating on how the conscious mind can affect the unconscious and work together to make any goal achievable (Wikipedia[35]).

(8) "Twenty years from now you will be more disappointed by the things you didn't do than the things you did, so throw off the bow lines, sail away from safe harbor, catch the trade winds in your sails, explore, dream, discover."—Mark Twain

1835–1910: Samuel Langhorne Clemens—pen name "Mark Twain"— was an American writer, entrepreneur, humorist, publisher, and lecturer. Two of his most famous books are *The Adventures of Tom Sawyer* and *The Adventures of Huckleberry Finn*. Keep in mind that back then there was no TV, radio, movies, or social media. The writing, printing, and distribution of stories to entertain took much more time and effort (Wikipedia)[36].

(9) "You can never cross the ocean until you have the courage to lose sight of the shore."—Christopher Columbus

1451–1506: Christopher Columbus is credited with discovering the "New World" of the Americas in 1492. He made four trips to the Caribbean and South America. He is credited or blamed for opening up the Americas to European colonization. His goal for his 1492 voyage was to find an alternate route to India. Think of the faith it took travel beyond the end of the world as it was known then. Also, think about the outcome. Was he a failure because he didn't find the route to India that he sought (Biography.com)[37]?

(10) "If you hear a voice within you say, 'You cannot paint,' then by all means, paint."—Vincent van Gogh

1853–1890: Vincent Willem van Gogh became one of the most famous and influential figures in Western art history. He was a tortured soul suffering from mental illnesses that eventually led to his tragic suicide.

In a decade he created over twenty-one hundred paintings, over eight hundred of which were oil based. At least three of the paintings have sold for adjusted prices of over $100 million each (Wikipedia)[38].

(11) "Go confidently in the direction of your dreams. Live the life you have imagined."—Henry David Thoreau

"Live your beliefs and you can turn the world around."—Henry David Thoreau

1817–1862: Henry David Thoreau was an American author, naturalist, and philosopher who promoted the benefits of simple living in harmony with nature. His views on civil disobedience and civil rights influenced Leo Tolstoy, Mahatma Gandhi, and Martin Luther King Jr. He used his notoriety as an author to speak out and write against slavery (Wikipedia)[39].

(12) "Believe that you can and you are halfway there."—Theodore Roosevelt

1858–1919: Theodore Roosevelt became the twenty-sixth president of the United States in 1901 after unexpectedly after William McKinley was assassinated. He won reelection in 1904. He fought for and made progress with breaking up big business monopolies, conservation efforts including setting aside two hundred million acres for national forests and reserves and received the Nobel Peace Prize for his negotiation efforts to end the Russo-Japanese war (History.com)[40].

(13) "If you are offered a ride on a rocket ship, don't ask what seat! Just get on."—Sheryl Sandberg

1969: Sheryl Sandberg is chief operating officer for Meta Platforms (formerly Facebook). She was vice president of online sales and operations for Google and involved with its philanthropic arm Google.org (Wikipedia)[41].

(14) "In order to succeed, your desire for success should be greater than your fear of failure."—Bill Cosby

1937: Bill Cosby is an Emmy Award–winning and Grammy Award–winning comedian and actor. He earned a PhD in education at the

University of Massachusetts, Amherst. During his portrayal of father figure Cliff Huxtable in the TV series *The Cosby Show* from 1985 to 1989, he gained the moniker of America's Dad. He also starred in multiple movies and other TV shows (Wikipedia)[42].

(15) "The person who says it cannot be done should get out of the way of the person doing it."—Chinese Proverb

"Be not afraid of growing slowly. Be afraid of standing still."—Chinese Proverb

Chinese proverbs have been around for hundreds of years. There are purported to be over twenty thousand of them. Many are used in current day communications and philosophical discussions (Wikipedia)[43].

(16) "Build your own dreams, or someone else will hire you to build theirs."—Farrah Gray

1984: Born Farrakhan Khalid Muhammad, Farrah is a successful businessman, investor, columnist, author, and motivational speaker. He was also listed number five on the Famous Black Entrepreneurs list[44].

(17) "Dream big and dare to fail."—Norman Vaughan

1905–2005: Norman Vaughan was a dog handler on Admiral Byrd's expedition to the South Pole in 1928 for the fifteen-hundred-mile journey across Antarctica. Just before his eighty-ninth birthday, he returned to Antarctica and climbed Mount Vaughan (named for him). He had planned to climb it again at age one hundred but never did. He is said to have lived his famous quote to "dream big and dare to fail" for his one hundred years (Ordinarypeoplecanwin.com)[45].

(18) "You may be disappointed if you fail, but you are doomed if you don't try."—Beverly Sills

1929–2007: Beverly Sills was a very successful opera star who made opera more mainstream to the public instead of only for the elite. She was dubbed America's Opera Queen in 1971 by *Time* magazine. She performed twenty-eight full-length operas over her career and paved the way for other American opera artists (IMDb.com)[46].

(19) "Either write something worth reading or do something worth writing."—Benjamin Franklin

1706-1790: Benjamin Franklin was publisher, statesman, scientist, author, diplomat, and one of the Founding Fathers of the United States of America. He helped draft the Declaration of Independence. He negotiated the Treaty of Paris in 1783 that ended the Revolutionary War. Along with his famous experiments with electricity, he also was a very successful businessman with his printing business and gave back with helping to found a library, hospital, and college (history.com)[47]

(20) "There is nothing impossible to those who try."—Alexander the Great

356 BC-323 BC: Alexander the Great, former king of Macedonia, was taught at a young age to read, write and play the lyre (a U-shaped string instrument kind of like a harp). When he was a teenager, his father hired for him as a tutor the famed philosopher Aristotle. During his thirteen-year reign, he conquered lands in the Middle East as a military commander and created one of the largest empires in history. He built cities in many of the lands he conquered and named them Alexandria (nationalgeographic.org)[48].

(21) "Success is not final; failure is not fatal. It is the courage to continue that counts."—Winston Churchill

1874-1965: Winston Churchill served as Britain's prime minister from 1940 to 1945 during World War II and again from 1951 to 1955. He is widely considered one of the greatest figures of the twentieth century and stood his ground opposing Hitler and helping to save the world's democracies from the German fascism during the war (Wikipedia)[49].

(22) "You are never too old to set another goal or dream a new dream."—Malala Yousafzai

1997: Malala Yousafzai is a Pakistani activist for female education. She was the youngest ever Nobel Prize laureate for her struggle against the oppression of children and young people and for the right to an education for all children (nobelprize.org)[50].

(23) "It is never too late to be what you might have been."—George Elliot

1819–1880: George Elliot—pseudonym of Mary Ann Cross—was a British Victorian era novelist and poet who developed the method of psychological analysis characteristic of modern literature (Britannica.com)[51].

(24) "Perfection is not attainable, but if we chase perfection, we can catch excellence."—Vince Lombardi

1913–1970: Vincent Thomas Lombardi was an American coach in the National Football League (NFL). His coaching skills helped his teams to a 73 percent regular season winning percentage and 90 percent for postseason games. He is thought of by many as the best sports coach of all times. The award given to the team that wins the Super Bowl each year is the Vince Lombardi trophy (Wikipedia)[52].

(25) "Change your thoughts and you change the world."—Norman Vincent Peale

1898–1993: Norman Vincent Peale was an American author best known for making popular the concept of positive thinking and wrote multiple self-help books, including *The Power of Positive Thinking*. Millions of copies of that book were sold, it was on the *New York Times* best-seller list for 186 consecutive weeks and has been translated into many other languages. President Ronald Reagan awarded Norman the Presidential Medal of Freedom, the highest civilian honor in the United States (Wikipedia)[53].

(26) "In the end, it's not the years in your life that count. It's the life in your years."—Abraham Lincoln

1809–1865: Abraham Lincoln was president of the United States from 1860 to 1865. In 1863, during the Civil War, he issued the Emancipation Proclamation, freeing slaves in the South. He was a practicing lawyer, and his law partner said of him "his ambition was a little engine that knew no rest." He lost two elections for congressman, lost two elections for senator, had a failed business, and suffered many personal losses during his life but still became a great historical figure who accomplished a tremendous amount of good (Whitehouse.gov and snopes.com)[54].

(27) "It always seems impossible until it is done."—Nelson Mandela

1918–2013: Nelson Rolihlahla Mandela was a South African civil rights proponent and opponent of apartheid—a practice of race segregation with preference to whites. He spent twenty-seven years in prison for having a dissenting opinion from the government. After he was released, he was elected the country's first black head of state in a democratic election. He worked to end apartheid and mend racial divisions. He was awarded the Nobel Peace Prize and is often referred to as the "Father of the Nation" (Wikipedia)[55].

(28) "Life isn't about finding yourself. Life is about creating yourself."—George Bernard Shaw

1856–1950: George Bernard Shaw was born in Ireland and was a successful prominent playwright author. He used his plays to attack what he saw as social hypocrisy. One of his more famous plays, *Pygmalion*, was about the attempt to change a local street woman with a cockney dialect into a proper speaking member of high society. He received the Nobel Prize for Literature in 1925 (Nobelprize.org)[56].

(29) "You must be the change you wish to see in the world." —Mahatma Gandhi

1869–1948: Mohandas Karamchand Gandhi was a lawyer, politician, social activist, and writer who became a social activist in India against the British rule of India. He was renowned for his nonviolent protest to achieve social change. He was considered by many of the people to be Mahatma or "Great Soul." His also called by many the "Father of His Country" (brittanica.com)[57].

(30) "Don't go through life; grow through life."—Eric Butterworth

1916–2003: Eric Butterworth was a leader in modern times of "practical mysticism." He helped thousands of people to help themselves live a more abundant life by the study and application of the truth. He was able to put complex metaphysical teachings into simple sound bites of awareness, hence the quote. To my knowledge, he was not related to the maple syrup icon (truthunity.net)[58].

(31) "If there is no struggle, there is not progress."—Frederick Douglas

1817–1895: Frederick Douglas was escaped from slavery in Maryland and became an author and activist in the anti-slavery abolitionist movement seeking to end slavery. Even after the Civil War and Emancipation Proclamation, he continued working toward equality and human rights. He was also a champion of women's rights, especially their right to vote (history.com)[59].

(32) "Do the best that you can until you know better. Then when you know better, be better."—Maya Angelou

1928–2014: Maya Angelou was an American poet, writer, and civil rights activist. She had multiple odd jobs in her early adulthood an became very successful in theater, movies, and television. She was active in the civil rights movement and worked with Martin Luther King Jr. Angelo recited her poem "On the Pulse of Morning" at Bill Clinton's first inaugural address (Wikipedia)[60].

(33) "Incredible change happens in your life when you decide to take control of what you have power over instead of craving control over what you don't."—Steve Maraboli

1975– Steve Maraboli is a motivational speaker, internet radio commentator, and author. He is a decorated veteran and philanthropist. *Inc.* magazine listed him as a "Top Leader to Follow" in 2016, and he has received the United Nations Award for Philanthropy (Wikiquotes and IMDb.com)[61].

(34) "What we fear most is usually what we most need to do." —Ralph Waldo Emerson

(35) "The purpose of life is not to be happy. It is to be useful, to be honorable, to be compassionate, to have it make some difference that you lived and lived well."—Ralph Waldo Emerson

(36) "What lies behind us and what lies ahead of us are tiny matters to what lies within us."—Ralph Waldo Emerson.

1803–1882: Ralph Waldo Emerson was an American writer, philosopher, and abolitionist. He led the Transcendentalist movement of the nineteenth century. He was a champion of individualism and did most his writing in the form of essays. He was also a key figure in the American Romantic Movement (Wikipedia)[62].

(37) "Someone is sitting in shade because someone planted a tree a long time ago."—Warren Buffet

1930: Warren Buffet is an American businessman, investor, and philanthropist. With a net financial worth of $105 billion as of November 2021, he is one of the ten wealthiest people in the world. He is considered one of the best investors alive. Buffet has pledged to give 99 percent of his wealth to charitable causes (Wikipedia)[63].

(38) "Life is like riding a bicycle. To keep your balance, you must keep moving."—Albert Einstein

(39) "Imagination is more important than knowledge. Knowledge is limited, imagination circles the world."—Albert Einstein

1879–1955: Albert Einstein began reading and studying science at an early age. He worked at a Swiss patent office, taught at universities, and continued his scientific studies. He contributed a great deal to the understanding of physics and how the universe works with the equation he developed, $E=MC^2$, and his theories on general and special relativity. Albert Einstein is considered by many to be one of the smartest people who ever lived (IMDb.com)[64].

(40) "We are all self-made, but only the successful will admit it." —Earl Nightingale

(41) "One hour per day of study in your chosen field is all it takes. One hour per day of will put you at the top of your field within three years. Within five years you'll be a national authority. In seven years, you can be one of the best people in the world at what you do."—Earl Nightingale

1921-1989: Earl Nightingale was an American radio speaker and author on the topics of personal growth, motivation, and success. He recorded over 7,000 radio programs and 250 audio training programs. Two of his more famous works are *The Strangest Secret* and *Lead the Field*. He said that he was motivated by Napoleon Hill's *Think and Grow Rich* book (Wikipedia)[65].

> (42) "I saw the angel in the marble and carved until I set him free." —Michelangelo

1475-1564: Michelangelo Buenarroti was an Italian painter, sculptor, and poet. He is considered to be one of the most brilliant artists of the Italian Renaissance. Two of his most famous works are the statue *David* and the painting on the Sistine chapel in Rome (biography.com)[66].

> (43) "The past is history, the future is a mystery, and this moment is a gift. That is why we call it the present."—Alice Morse Earle

1853-1911: Alice Morse Earle was an American author who wrote about colonial history. She wrote extensively about the manners and customs of colonial New England and New York. She tended to write more about the details of colonial living instead of the larger picture (Historyswomen.com and Wikipedia)[67].

> (44) "When you want something bad enough, all the universe conspires in helping you achieve it."—Paulo Coelho

1947: Paulo Coehlo is a Brazilian author and lyricist. His novel *The Alchemist* is the most successful book ever by a Brazilian writer, with sales of over $150 million. Before becoming an author, he worked as actor, journalist, and theater director (Wikipedia)[68].

> (45) "We all possess more power and greater possibilities than we realize and visualizing is one of the greatest. In visualizing, or making a mental picture, you are not endeavoring to change the laws of nature. You ae fulfilling them."—Genevieve Behrend.

1847–1916: Genevieve Behrend was the only student of Thomas Troward, the "Master of Mental Science." Her book *Your Invisible Power* remains one of the best-selling books about mental science of all times. French born, she established and ran schools in New York City and Los Angeles. She reached millions by radio and had tens of thousands of students across the world (wwwhubs.com)[69].

(46) "Anyone who stops learning is old, whether twenty or eighty. Anyone who keeps learning stays young. The greatest thing in life is to keep your mind young."—Henry Ford

1863–1947: Henry Ford was an American industrialist who revolutionized manufacturing by developing the assembly line production method. He helped transform America into the industrial superpower it is today. He is credited with "Fordism," the mass production of inexpensive goods with high wages for workers (Brittanica.com and Wikipedia)[70].

(47) "A candle never loses any of its light while lighting another candle."—Rumi

1207–1273: Rumi was a Persian poet and mystic from the region of now Afghanistan. He had a history of love, longing, and loss that inspired him to express himself in poetry. His philosophy is that light should be a journey to union with the one true God, which is achieved by practicing love (Wikipedia and Britannica.com)[71].

(48) "If you can't fly, then run. If you can't run, then walk. If you can't walk, then crawl. Whatever you do, you have to keep moving forward."—Martin Luther King Jr.

1929–1968: Martin Luther King Jr. was an American Baptist minister and civil rights activist. He advanced civil rights with his inspirational speeches, nonviolent protests, and civil disobedience demonstrations. One of his more famous speeches was "I Have a Dream" at the Lincoln Memorial. He was inspired by the nonviolent approach of Gandhi (Wikipedia)[72].

Chapter Summary

- Learn and be inspired by people who have done great things.
- Avail yourself of the wisdom of the ages.
- Pay attention to what others have to say and who they are or were.
- Feed your mind and soul with knowledge and wisdom, and you will grow in both.
- For what wisdom or quote will you be remembered?

Conclusion

a. We are all capable of greatness!
b. You are in control of your situation, especially your attitude!
c. What doing-better goals are worthy of your efforts?
d. The only real failure is not trying at all.
e. Intention to change is not change! You must do!

We are magical beings, are we not? We create things from nothing with our imagination, ideas, dreams, and goals. We communicate with each other over vast distances. We have traveled to the moon and sent probes to other planets and beyond. We have built the internet, social media platforms, and have access to information and each other like never before. We have access to the world's knowledge at the tip of our fingers. We have tremendous power over our lives, vast opportunities, and more tools to set and achieve our goals, do better, and be better. We have control over our lives and can affect the lives of others like no other time in history. The key to everything is you. You are in the wonderful place of having so many opportunities in front of you at the best time in history to learn and to connect with others. I sincerely hope that you have gained some valuable insight, knowledge, tips, tactics, and/or motivation to do better from this book.

We all know that what we eat and drink can have short- and long-term effects on our bodies. When we can, we try to eat right, drink enough water, maybe take vitamins. Many of us exercise at least occasionally if not regularly and pretty much agree that it is good for our health. How often do you think about what you feed your mind, spirit, or soul? How often do you exercise your mind, spirit, or soul? Instead of watching TV or movies, scrolling though Facebook posts, reading and writing tweets, or spending time on TikTok or YouTube, how about looking up things you want to know about on the internet, researching positive quotes, reading a self-help or inspirational book or an e-book, or actually going out and doing something that expands your experiences? Write down some goals, and draft some behaviors you can do to reach them. Research online how to better yourself, and reach out to people who can help you. Longer term, how about volunteering a few hours a week to a good cause and being around people doing the same, starting your own blog, writing a book, or starting a nonprofit group to do good works? Good for you for somehow getting a copy of this book and hopefully taking some steps to do better. Your future is in your hands.

As you go forward on your wonderous journey of life remember to:

a. Have dreams, ambitions, and goals, and write them down.
b. Understand why you want and keep your desire strong.
c. Control and keep your attitude positive.
d. Stop doing the wrong things.
e. Break your goals into manageable steps.
f. Learn from setbacks and failures.
g. Deal better with crises and find opportunities in them.
h. Keep in mind why others act and their needs.
i. Serve others and their needs and you will succeed.
j. Give yourself credit for making progress.
k. Give yourself a break if you get something wrong or make a mistake.
l. Get up at least one more time than you fall.
m. Enjoy the work, the learning, the progress, and even the setbacks.
n. You don't have to do great and be great, you get to!

I am excited for you and the opportunities that you have to achieve your goals and greatness. If you found any benefit in reading this book, please share what you have learned with others so that they may benefit as well. As you begin to do better and be better, please consider doing a minor act that combined with others can have a huge benefit and help a lot of other people to do better and be better. Please purchase at least two more copies of this book and give them to people you think might best benefit from it. Maybe a colleague, friend, neighbor, niece, nephew, or another person.

You could leave a couple of copies at work for others, at an airport, train station, or at a church. The hope is that you can do better, be better, and help others be better!

As you work your way on your journey, sometimes it helps to refresh and remind yourself why you are on the path you are and what it is that you want. We reach our goals, change our minds, and decide to do something different and sometimes feel like we need a refresh or boost. We are not always on track, driven, clear of purpose, or fired up about what we are doing at any given time. The great thing about that is that we have the ability to assess how things are going, find tools to do better, improve, and go on. Along with reviewing the bulleted items earlier in this chapter, consider reviewing the following items from time to time as a reminder of many of the major points in this book:

- Why do anything?
- Don't you deserve to do better?
- Isn't it time you started doing better?
- What do you want? What are your dreams? You get to choose what you want.
- The key to everything is your attitude! Happiness is an attitude.
- You have control over your attitude. Make it real!
- Write down your dreams and goals. Give yourself a time frame. Do it and do it better!
- Take steps and get things done.
- The more you do, the better you are doing. Stop doing the wrong things!
- Break your bad habits that are holding you back.

- You know some things you should stop doing, so stop doing them. Start doing the right things!
- Create new positive behavior goals.
- Take the right steps, and do something daily when you can.
- Do better with better choices.
- Deal better with crises.
- You will get through your next crisis, well or poorly, it is up to you.
- In every crisis, there is opportunity.
- Keep balance and enjoy the journey.
- Things do not work well when out of balance, neither do you.
- It is not all about the destination; enjoy the journey along the way. Deal better with people.
- The business of business is people.
- Follow The Platinum Rule: Do unto others as they would have done unto them!
- Make it happen!
- You are the one who will make things happen.
- As you serve others better, you will do and be better. Use wisdom and inspiration from others.
- Learn from and be inspired by those who have gone before you.
- Feed your mind, your heart, and your soul with knowledge, wisdom, and hope.
- Help pay it forward!
- If you do better and provide more for others, you will do better and be better.
- Pass on your knowledge, inspire someone to do better, and share copies of this book.

Remember: you are the master of your own destiny. You write your own script. If it is to be, it is up to you. Things don't just happen for you. You have to work for them. Think about it; do you really want to win the lottery? Would it not also present its own problems with all that money? Isn't success worked for much more satisfying? When my wife reads what I said about the lottery she will think that I am insane. Yes, it would be nice to have all that cash to do a lot of good and enjoy ourselves for a while, but I worry that it would change us and our priorities. Don't get me wrong; if we win a Mega Millions or Powerball, I don't plan to refuse it. I will make the best of it and try to grow positively with the changes. For now, I will continue to work hard where I can and use the tools that I can to stay motivated and productive while carving out the successes within my power. There is a story I heard about a man who used to pray week in and week out to win the lottery. Eventually, God answered him and said, "Meet me halfway and at least buy a ticket!" To have a chance at winning the lottery, you have to at least buy a ticket. To succeed in life, you have to try!

To remind yourself of your goals and dreams, you might use consider creating a vision board and keeping it nearby for you to look at. Post simple lists of dreams, goals, and aspirations. I have a list of about two dozen positive things and accomplishments posted on a filing cabinet that I turn and look at occasionally. When thinking about your goals and dreams, pick one on which you can concentrate. What will it look like when you achieve it? What will it sound like? What will it feel like? What will it smell like?

What will it taste like (or what will your first meal after reaching your goal taste like?) I have an idea for what this book will look like when published. I imagine what the sound will be when I flip the pages. The hard cover will crack a bit the first time I fully open one. It will have that new book smell. I can taste the prime rib I will eat at my celebration party.

If you are planning on writing a book, be sure to prepare yourself for a potential long haul of multiple submissions, rejections, or just not hearing back. Expect to make mistakes, learn from them, and do better. Together with others who partnered with me in writing this book, we share the general concept of being better and doing better, and hopefully will make a great positive impact. As you strive to do better and be better, you will do both. Confucius said, "The man who says he can and the man who says he cannot, are both correct." Set your heart on your dreams and goals, believe you can, do the work, and look out, world, because nothing is going to stop you!

I am eager to hear your comments about what portions of this book you found most helpful. Please let me know if you have had any success from some of the ideas or tactics from the book. If you want to share your thoughts on this book or how I might be able to do better with the next one, please send me an email at: MEbetterbook@gmail.com. Feel free to be candid with your comments and suggestions; however, keep in mind that what will really help me with the next book is what you found helpful, other things to add to do better, any success you have had from reading this book and messages, and thoughts or ideas you think would help others.

- Enjoy the wonderous ride of life and all your opportunities!
- Don't be afraid to want, desire, maybe fail, then keep going and succeed!
- There are a lot of forces, people, knowledge, and wisdom to help you achieve greatness!
- You are stronger than you know, can get through any trial, and accomplish any dream!
- Do learn, enjoy, help others along the way, and feel great while doing it!

Appendices

Appendix 1—Talents People Have

1. Ability to deal with failure
2. Ability to focus
3. Ability to handle change
4. Ability to make friends
5. Ability to spot new trends
6. Abstract thinking
7. Academics
8. Accounting
9. Acrobatics
10. Acting
11. Adaptability
12. Advertising
13. Advising
14. Appraising
15. Appreciation
16. Affiliate systems
17. Analyzing the past
18. Archery
19. Architecture

20. Arguing
21. Art
22. Articulating
23. Asking questions
24. Astrology
25. Astronomy
26. Athleticism
27. Awareness
28. Baking
29. Banking
30. Bargain hunting
31. Bargaining
32. Bidding
33. Blacksmithing
34. Blogging
35. Board games
36. Boat racing
37. Bookkeeping
38. Boxing
39. Brainstorming
40. Brewing
41. Bridge-building
42. Budgeting
43. Building
44. Calligraphy
45. Card making
46. Carpentry
47. Cartography

48. Carving pumpkins
49. Charming people
50. Cheering people up
51. Cleaning
52. Climbing
53. Comforting others
54. Communication
55. Composing music
56. Computer coding
57. Computers/IT
58. Conflict resolution
59. Construction
60. Cooking
61. Coping
62. CPR
63. Crafts
64. Creativity
65. Crisis management
66. Critical thinking
67. Dancing
68. Daycare
69. Dealing with people
70. Debating
71. Decision-making
72. Defending
73. Dentistry
74. Designing
75. Detail orientation

76. Dexterity
77. Diagnosing illness
78. Directing
79. Disguising oneself
80. Disposal
81. Dispute resolution
82. Dog care
83. Drama
84. Drawing
85. Dressmaking
86. Driving
87. Editing
88. Electronics
89. Empathy
90. Encouraging
91. Enthusiasm
92. Estimating
93. Fairness
94. Farming
95. Fashion
96. Fighting
97. Financial management
98. Financial planning
99. Finding things
100. Firefighting
101. Fishing
102. Fixing things
103. Flying a plane

104. Following
105. Forgiving
106. Future thinking
107. Futurism
108. Gambling
109. Gardening
110. Gathering
111. Gem-cutting
112. Getting people to tell their secrets
113. Gift wrapping
114. Giving good massages
115. Governing
116. Graphic design
117. Graphics
118. Graphics arts
119. Guerrilla marketing
120. Hairstyling
121. Health/Fitness
122. Herbology
123. Herding sheep
124. High energy
125. Hiking
126. Hiring/Recruiting
127. Horse training
128. Horseback riding
129. House renovations
130. Human resources
131. Humor

132. Hunting
133. Hypnotizing
134. Ice skating
135. Identify strengths
136. Imagination
137. Initiative
138. Innovation
139. Inspiring
140. Integrity/Honesty
141. Interior decorating
142. Interpreting
143. Intuition
144. Inventiveness
145. Investigating
146. Investing
147. Jewelry-making
148. Keeping secrets
149. Knitting
150. Knot-making
151. Landscaping
152. Lawn care
153. Leadership
154. Leading business meetings
155. Learner
156. Learning foreign languages
157. Leatherworking
158. Legal
159. Lip reading

160. Listening
161. Logic
162. Logistics
163. Magic
164. Maintenance
165. Making connections
166. Marketing
167. Mathematics
168. Mechanic
169. Medicine
170. Meeting management
171. Memorizing things
172. Mending
173. Mentoring
174. Metal work
175. Mining
176. Model making
177. Modeling
178. Money management
179. Motivating
180. Movie reviews
181. Music
182. Navigating
183. Negotiating
184. Networking with people
185. Organizing
186. Origami
187. Painting

188. Palm reading
189. Parenting
190. People judgment
191. Persistence
192. Personal productivity
193. Persuading people
194. Pest control
195. Philosophy
196. Photo or video editing
197. Photography
198. Photoshop
199. Physics
200. Planning
201. Playing a musical instrument
202. Playing chess
203. Plotting
204. Plumbing
205. Poetry
206. Polyglot (many languages)
207. Positiveness
208. Pottery
209. Predicting the weather
210. Preparing
211. Prioritizing
212. Problem-solving
213. Programming
214. Project management
215. Public speaking

216. Publishing
217. Questioning
218. Racing
219. Raising money
220. Reading
221. Reasoning
222. Relaxation
223. Reliability
224. Relieve stress
225. Remembering
226. Repairing things
227. Representing
228. Researching
229. Rhyming
230. Risk management
231. Roofing
232. Running
233. Safecracking
234. Sailing
235. Sales
236. Scrapbooking
237. Seeing long distances
238. Self-control
239. Self-management
240. Self-assurance
241. Self-discipline
242. Sewing
243. Shooting

244. Shopping
245. Sign language
246. Singing
247. Social intelligence
248. Social media
249. Social networking
250. Software
251. Solving crimes
252. Speed-reading
253. Spelling
254. Sports
255. Spying
256. Storytelling
257. Strategic planning
258. Strategy games
259. Supporting
260. Surgery
261. Surveying
262. Surviving
263. Sympathy
264. Systems management
265. Taxes
266. Teaching
267. Training
268. Technology
269. Telling jokes
270. Theorizing
271. Time management

272. Tolerating
273. Translating
274. Troubleshooter
275. Typing
276. Typography
277. Video creation
278. Visualization
279. Volunteering
280. Waiting tables
281. Walking silently
282. Website development
283. Welding
284. Whistling
285. Winemaking
286. Wisdom
287. Woodworking
288. Wrestling
289. Writing

Appendix 2—Good Deed Ideas

1. Feed a homeless person.
2. Donate blankets and/or coats to a homeless shelter in the winter.
3. Order a pizza and send to a friend without taking credit.
4. At a toll, pay for the person behind you.
5. Put $100 in a blank envelope and leave it for someone you know is struggling.
6. Share some helpful wisdom with a child.
7. Leave positive/inspiring post it notes around the house.
8. Donate to a charity.

9. Give someone a compliment.
10. Anonymously send someone flowers.
11. Bring your old magazines to a doctor's office or hospital waiting area.
12. Register as an organ donor.
13. Donate old books to a library.
14. Write a thank-you note to a company that treated you well.
15. Call someone you wronged and apologize.
16. Ask to see the manager at a restaurant and tell them "great job" when appropriate.
17. Sponsor a child's wish through the Make-a-wish Foundation.
18. Leave a gift on a stranger's doorstep.
19. Pay for someone's expired parking meter.
20. Do a task around the house your spouse or roommate normally does.
21. Reward someone for a good deed they did.
22. Leave a nice thank-you note and/or an extra-large tip for a waiter or waitress.
23. Share an inspirational quote you heard.
24. Volunteer for a cause or event.
25. Donate old clothes and/or furniture to a charity (often they will pick up at your place).
26. Write a letter to troop(s) serving.
27. Learn CPR.
28. Call and report the next time you see an impaired or unsafe driver.
29. Donate blood.
30. Register as an organ donor.
31. Reach out to someone you heard is sick and offer to help.

32. Leave money at a vending machine or gas pump.
33. Pick up litter as you walk by it.
34. Let someone go in front of you in line.
35. Make an extra effort to hold a door open for someone.
36. Offer to carry something for someone.
37. When you go shopping, ask someone you know if they need anything.
38. Participate in a fundraiser.
39. Cook a special meal for someone.
40. Send a handwritten thank-you letter instead of a text.
41. Bring in donuts for coworkers.
42. Help a child or older person cross the street.
43. Perform random acts of kindness.
44. Tell someone. "Good job."
45. Tell a family member you appreciated them.
46. Send an encouraging text.
47. Intercede with a bully.
48. Mentor a child.
49. Next time you feel like bad-mouthing someone, don't.
50. Let someone go before you in traffic.
51. Thank your editor for being awesome.
52. Encourage someone's new idea.
53. Reach out and contact someone you heard had a crisis.
54. Leave an "I love you" note.
55. Next time you feel like you are about to do something wrong, don't do it.
56. Pick up and throw away trash when you walk by it.

57. Do good deed ideas from Goodnet.org and Random Acts of Kindness.org.
58. Commit to being less angry.
59. Do a little better each day with something.
60. Set noble goals, and take steps to achieve them.
61. Report child abuse.
62. Report a drunk driver.
63. Confront a friend or family member about their self-destructive behavior.
64. Volunteer time at a local charity.
65. Apologize to someone you wronged in the past.
66. Give up your seat to someone on a train.
67. Mow the lawn, shovel snow, or rake leaves for a neighbor.
68. Offer to work a shift for a coworker.
69. Next time you feel the need to yell at someone, yell "Thank you!" or "Good luck!"
70. Leave money at a friend's house anonymously.
71. Tell someone you think they are gifted and why.
72. Buy a lottery ticket and give it away.
73. Buy lunch for a colleague.
74. Show appreciation when warranted.
75. Tell someone they are your favorite.
76. Next time you want to tell an insensitive joke, don't.
77. Win your next argument by avoiding it.
78. Buy and donate socks or gloves to a homeless shelter.

79. Ask someone when they are down if they need a hug.
80. Tell someone you think they are awesome.
81. Tell someone today will be a great day!
82. When you have a chance, be a hero!

Endnotes

1. Ralph Waldo Emerson – collective conscious - https://en.wikipedia.org/wiki/ralph_waldo_emerson
2. Hill, Napoleon, *Think & Grow Rich*, 2008 edition by Barnes & Noble, Inc., New York
3. Bill Gates Inc on Line - https://www.inc.com/marcel-schwantes/bill-gates-success-leadership-skill.html
4. Elon Musk – https://www.entrepreneur.com/leadership/what-skills-does-elon-musk-have-and-why-is-he-so-successful/371552
5. Jeff Bezos – https://www.cnbc.com/2018/05/02/jeff-bezos-this-is-what-you-are-going-to-regret-at-80.html
6. Oprah Winfrey – https://www.entrepreneur.com/starting-a-business/24-quotes-on-success-from-oprah-winfrey/269979
7. Michael Jordan – https://willnevergiveup.com/Michael-jordan-succeed-must-learn-failure
8. Austin Russell – https://www.forbes.com/sites/alanohnsman/2020/12/03/meet-the-worlds-newest-and-youngest-self-made-billionaire-luminars-austin-russell/?sh=43bbf168123b
9. Aristotle https://lifehacker.com/we-are-what-we-repeatedly-do-5946348
10. Hill, Napoleon, *Think & Grow Rich*, 2008 edition by Barnes & Noble, Inc., New York

11. William Shakespeare https://nosweatshakespeare.com/quotes/famous/the-worlds-your-oyster/#:~:text=%27The%20world%20is%20your%20oyster%27%20origin&text=The%20actual%20quote%20is%20%27The,women%20out%20of%20their%20money.
12. Maslow's hierarchy of needs https://en.wikipedia.org/wiki/maslow%27_hierarchy_of_needs
13. Maslow Hierarchy of Needs Chart https://en.wikipedia.org/wiki/maslow%27_hierarchy_of_needs
14. Amelia Earhart https://www.goodreads.com/quotes/123820
15. W. Clement Stone https://www.brainyquotes/w_clement_stone_193777
16. Friedrich Nietzsche https://www.dictionary.com/e/slang/what-doesnt-kill-you-makes-you-stronger
17. Wikipedia Zero Sum Game https://en.wikipedia.org/wiki/Zero-sum_game
18. Hard lessons web site https://www.powerofpositivity.com/hard-lessons-people-learn-life/
19. TQM – Pharmatutor – Pharmacy Infopedia https://www.pharmatutor.org/articles/concept-philosophy-total-quality-management
20. Deming's 14 points - Pharmacy Infopedia https://www.pharmatutor.org/articles/concept-philosophy-total-quality-management
21. Definition of optimism on line – https://www.bing.com/search?q=define+optimism&FORM=DCTSRC
22. 5 reasons to be more optimistic https://www.verywellmind.com/unbelievable-facts-about-optimists-1717551
23. Life Optimizer best 10 of 45 benefits of optimism https://www.lifeoptimizer.org/2010/03/04/benefits-of-optimism
24. Freedictionary.com
    a – https//www.thefreedictionary.com/inspiration
    b – https//www.thefreedictionary.com/motivation

25. Keydifferences.com https://keydifferences.com/difference-between-motivation-and-inspiration.html

26. Willpower – https://www.merriam-webster.com/dictionary/willpower

27. Procrastinate – https://merriam-webster.com/dictionary/procrastinate

28. Types of fears https://fearlessliving.org/types-of-fear

29. Utilize definition https://eliteediting.com/resources/use-vs-utilize/#...

30. Albert Schweitzer bio https://www.encyclopedia.com/people/philosophy-and-religion/protestant-christianity-biographies/albert-schweitzer

31. Dale Carnegie bio https://www.britanica.com/Dale-Carnegie

32. Thomas Jefferson bio https://monticello.org-thomas-jefferson/

33. Jim Rohn bio https://en.wikipedia.org/wiki/Jim_Rohn

34. Bruce Lee bio https://wikipedia.org/wiki/Bruce_Lee

35. Napoleon Hill bio https://en.wikipedia.org/wiki/Napoleon_Hill

36. Samuel Langhorne Clemens bio https://en.wikipedia.org/wiki/Mark_Twain

37. Christopher Columbus bio https://www.biography.com/history-culture/christopher-columbus

38. Vincent Van Goh bio https://en.wikipedia.org/wiki/Vincent_van_Gogh

39. Henry David Thoreau bio https://en.wikipedia.org/wiki/Henry_David_Thoreau

40. Theodore Roosevelt bio https://www.history.com/topics/us-presidents/theodore-roosevelt

41. Sheryl Sandberg bio https://en.wikipedia.org/wiki/Sheryl_Sandberg

42. Bill Cosby bio https://en.wikipedia.org/wiki/Bill_Cosby

43. Chinese proverbs https://en.wikipedia.org/wiki/Chinese_proverbs
44. Farrah Gray bio https://www.history.com/topics/american-revolution/benjamin-franklin
45. Norman Vaughan bio https://ordinarypeoplecanwin.com/WhereSeldom.htm
46. Beverly Sills bio https://www.imdb.com/name/nm0798116/
47. Benjamin Franklin bio https://www.history.com/topics/american-revolution/benjamin-franklin
48. Alexander the Great bio https://www.nationalgeographic.org/encyclopedia/alexander-great
49. Winston Churchill bio https://en.wikipedia.org/wiki/Winston_Churchill
50. Malala Yousafzai bio https://www.nobelprize.org/prizes/peace/2014/yousafzai
51. George Elliot bio https://www.britannica.com/biography/George-Eliot
52. Vincent Lombardi bio https://en.wikipedia.org/wiki/Vince_Lombardi
53. Norman Vincent Peale bio https://en.wikipedia.org/wiki/Norman_Vincent_Peale
54. Abraham Lincoln bio https://www.snopes.com/fact-check/abraham-lincoln-failure/?collection=407579
55. Nelson Mandela bio https://en.wikipedia.org/wiki/Nelson_Mandela
56. George Bernard Shaw bio https://www.nobelprize.org/literature/1925/shaw/facts
57. Mohandas Karamchand Gandhi bio https://www.brittanica.com/Mahatma-Gandhi
58. Eric Butterworth bio https://truthunity.net/people/eric-butterworth

59. Frederick Douglas bio https://www.history.com/topics/black-history/frederick-douglas

60. Maya Angelou bio https://simple.wikipedia.org/wiki/Maya_Angelou

61. Steve Maraboli bio https://en.wikiquute.org/wike/Steve_Maraboli & https://www.imdb.com/name/nm344059/bio

62. Ralph Waldo Emerson bio https://en.wikipedia.org/wiki/Ralph_Waldo_Emerson

63. Warren Buffet bio https://en.wikipedia.org/wiki/Warrent_Buffet

64. Albert Einstein bio http://www.imdb.com/name/nm0251868

65. Earl Nightingale bio https://en.wikipedia.org/Earl_Nightingale

66. Michelangelo Buonarroti bio https://www.biography.com/artists/michelangelo

67. Alice Morse Earle bio https://www.historyswomen.com/early-america/alicepmorse-earle and https://en.wikipedia.org/wiki/Alice_Morse_Earle

68. Paulo Coelho bio https://en.wikipedia.org/wiki/Paulo_Coelho

69. Genevieve Behrend bio https://genevievbehrend.wwwhubshubs.com

70. Henry Ford bio https://www.brittanica.com/biography/Henry-Ford and http://en.wikipedia.org/wiki/Henry_Ford

71. Rumi bio https://en.wikipedia.org/wiki/Rumi and https://www.brittanica.com/biography/Runi

72. Martin Luther King, Jr. bio https://en.wikipedia.org/wiki/Martin_Luther_King_Jr.

www.ingramcontent.com/pod-product-compliance
Lightning Source LLC
Chambersburg PA
CBHW070057080526
44586CB00013B/1091